The Fractured Phoenix

Gifts From a Broken Childhood

Wendy Lynn Wolfe

Blue Sun Studio, Inc.

The Fractured Phoenix
by Wendy Lynn Wolfe

ISBN: 978-0-9991960-0-7

Contents

Dedication

To Lynn Rose and all the brave children who live within us.

How to Use This Book

This book is divided into five parts. The first part is primarily my story with lessons I've learned. The remaining parts of the book are more informational in nature (and still have stories), providing you with a variety of techniques and processes to assist you in your healing and energy management.

If you are currently experiencing flashbacks or Post Traumatic Stress Disorder, be aware that you might be triggered by what is written in Chapters 1 and 3. I purposely did not go into significant detail about the abuse I experienced to avoid triggering readers. However, if you feel uncomfortable at any point (hyperventilating, tense muscles, intrusive images, feeling separate from your body), I suggest you stop reading and seek guidance from a trauma professional. This is also true if you experience any of these sensations while trying out a suggested exercise or meditation.

Part Two will help you understand how your early childhood experiences have changed the way you use your personal energy, how this affects your body and relationships, and what you can do to restore your vitality. Following the suggestions and processes, you will find significant relief from the energy challenges, overwhelm, and the stress on your physical body. You will also learn in this part the incredible power of your open heart.

In Part Three, you will learn about the many gifts of your experiences and in Part Four, how to tap into the gifts. I've given you all the basic information I provide in my animal communication and energy related workshops. While it isn't a substitute for actually attending a workshop, it's a great start with many tools to use.

Because there are many ways in which people refer to the unseen "Source of all," I have chosen to use the term God or Source. If you are more comfortable with Goddess, Spirit, The Great Mystery, Great Spirit, Allah or any other term, please substitute in your mind that which is most comfortable for you.

My experience is working with women and I wrote this book for women, but men have also experienced trauma and many are affected in similar ways as are mentioned in this book.

To provide privacy to my previous partners, I have changed their names in this book.

Introduction

THE FIRST TIME I worked earnestly at writing this book I was struck ill with Lymes Disease. I was so exhausted; taking a shower was an achievement. After a year of healing, I was ready to get back to my book. After four days of writing, I began experiencing excruciating back pain. I hadn't done anything strenuous, yet somehow a disc in my back became herniated, making it impossible for me to sit or stand at a computer. After three months of lying on my back and side, heavily medicated, I opted for surgery and was able to get back to my previous abilities.

The connection between the book and the illnesses preventing me from writing was not lost on me. This book is my "me too." I am breaking the silence. I will no longer keep the secret of my early childhood experience.

Though I'm quite certain all of the perpetrators are either dead or very feeble, the child who lives within me is still terrified. Her fear can create havoc in my body. My child self knew what they were capable of, because she endured horrendous acts of abuse and torture. She believed her perpetrators when they told her they had supernatural powers and could find her anywhere to destroy her beloved pets and family.

I am speaking my truth despite the disbelief of some family members. Even though my oldest sister was diagnosed with multiple personality disorder (also known as Dissociative Identity Disorder), which always is the result of extensive childhood trauma, her story and mine have been met with disbelief by my mother and other sisters. Before his death, my father denied his involvement.

This book isn't only about my story and my secret. The other secret exposed in this book is the one which will interest you the most. The other secret is that for those of us who have walked through the fire early in this lifetime, the veil (or doorway) to the Spirit dimension is often much thinner than we realize. We can more readily access our intuitive and psychic abilities than others.

What I mean by "walking through the fire" is early experiences of trauma, whether it is psychological, physical, sexual, or from having been the child of alcoholic/substance abuser parents. Trauma may have been intentional by others, such as neglect and abuse, or it may be the result of illness, premature birth or trauma in the womb, death of a parent or sibling, or mental illness in the family.

As hard as it may seem to comprehend, there is a gift inherent in our experiences. We learned at an early age how to sense energy and we tend to be *more intuitive* and *more energetically sensitive*. Without understanding these attributes, we can experience struggle and pain, both physical and emotional. Once we begin to see the *gift* and learn to use our abilities, our sensitivities give us greater insight, clairvoyance, and power in the world.

Our early life fire is reminiscent of the myth of Phoenix Rising, but with our own unique twist. You and I are the Fractured Phoenix. We are creating our own myth through our courageous stories of triumph from trauma. In the old myth of the Phoenix, after a long life of 500 to 1000 years, the Phoenix gathers aromatic boughs and spices of cinnamon, spikenard, and myrrh and builds a nest which ignites, engulfing the Phoenix in flames. Yet the Phoenix does not die. Death is an illusion. The physical body is destroyed and transforms into a new young bird rising from the ashes. The Phoenix continues to live for another 500-1000 years.

In our new myth, we, the Fractured Phoenixes burned in the fire of abuse and are reborn, but because of our early life experiences, we have fractures which require healing before we can take flight. Then, when we heal and take flight, we fly higher than had we never been fractured. There is extraordinary strength and bountiful gifts in our healed fractures.

In the original myth, before the Phoenix takes its first flight, it builds an egg of myrrh, placing the ashes from its own inferno within the egg, and then it takes flight to deliver it to the altar of the Sun God. Using myrrh to build the egg is significant, because myrrh is often associated with tears. Myrrh is harvested by piercing the myrrh bush, causing reddish drops of liquid to bleed out, hardening into tear-shaped drops. The Fractured Phoenix places her past inside this "casing of tears" to be purified.

Creating the egg is symbolic for how we can take the experiences and tears of our past, the abuse, the trauma, the shame, the guilt, and the feelings of betrayal, and place them in the container of the myrrh egg. Delivering the egg to the altar of the Sun God represents the handing over of our wounds and fractures to a higher power or God/Source. This key component to our healing releases us from our past while still honoring our journey. We acknowledge there was purpose in our past, but we are no longer defined by our experience.

The egg also represents wholeness. When we can honor the past, and embrace the gifts, we can feel whole (though we were never really broken). We can accept all of our life circumstances as part of who we are.

As we rise from the fire, we must heal our fractures in order to fly again. The fractures themselves, as well as the process of healing them, create a deeper sense of compassion for us and others. We begin to discover the false sense of separation from others. We become keenly aware of the connection between all beings. Our fire exercised and developed our intuitive, empathic, and healing gifts. We are more energetically sensitive and in tune with the world around us. Our empathic abilities allow us to sense pain in others, causing us to care deeply for the wellbeing of all. Through the healing of our fractures, we are able to embrace our intuitive and energetic gifts.

We are the heroes, not the victims. And because of our ability to rise out of the ashes and heal our fractures, we are among the ones our world needs most. We have risen out of the worst of the worst- torture, trauma, abuse, grave illness, abandonment and humiliation, often by the hands of a loved or trusted one. We have endured the most difficult of initiations to enhance our connection to Spirit. We understand pain and have gained the compassion required to witness and help alleviate it in others. We are here to be a reminder to others of the destruction wrought by neglect, control, fear, and anger. We are here to lift humanity up from the darkness of our imaginary separation from each other.

Our initiation is only the beginning. In order to fulfill our true and collective mission, we must first heal our fractures by recognizing and changing the emotional and energetic patterns we learned from our fire. We can then understand the truth of our experience, not the lies we came to believe about ourselves and our worth. We are not damaged goods. We are not "overly sensitive." We are not helpless victims. We can learn to deeply love and appreciate ourselves for what we endured. We can FEEL the heat of the fire, heal our fractures and rise from it as our life calling. We can learn to manage our valiant energy and embrace our gifts so we can fulfill our destiny.

Each of us is being called to find our way, and our own gifts, whether they are of healing, intuitive arts, or other callings. We each have something unique to unearth from the ashes. Our joy comes from discovering our distinctive gifts and offering them to the world.

What we lost in the fire, we will find in the ashes.

Part 1

Revealing My Story & Lessons

"The paradox of trauma is that it has both the power to destroy and the power to transform and resurrect."
—Peter A. Levine, PhD, In An Unspoken Voice

1

A Tribe of Perpetrators

THE MEMORIES I CHOSE to save from my childhood served me well. They allowed me to believe I grew up in a relatively normal family. They allowed me to function in the world. The memories I repressed for 30 years needed to be repressed. The only way I could survive the fire of my childhood was to bury the horrific memories deep within my psyche.

Most of what I remembered before age 10 revolves around playing with friends, spending long days in the arboretum with my sisters and being in school. Nature and animals surrounded and nurtured me. I could spend all day hiking the woods of the arboretum, stopping for lunch at a spring where I drank the cool, fresh water and picking the watercress for my "salad" to accompany the peanut butter sandwich I carried. These moments of calm and peace were my salvation from the darker reality I faced in my home life.

The memories of my home life are not as clear. On the fun side, I remember my father teaching me to swim, and taking me to outdoor movies in the station wagon with a big paper bag full of popcorn my mother made. There were occasions when we would get all the fixings for ice cream sundaes and laugh together while we ate our decadent creations. My mother would dance the car by pumping the brake (while making us promise not to tell Dad). We often sang silly songs while taking trips.

And there were the animals. The bunnies nesting in the bushes, the possums and raccoons at night, the deer, squirrels, and birds that surrounded us provided me a deep feeling of connection with all creatures. We always had pets: cats, dogs, guinea pigs, and hamsters. I loved our pets and relied upon them for comfort. We understood each other. We felt each other. They were safe.

There were other memories I wanted to forget. My father's temper could be explosive. I remember one incident when I was eight years old. I got up from the dining room table and the chair fell behind me. I hadn't intended for the chair to drop over; it was an accident, but my father accused me of intentionally pushing the chair over. He began yelling and I trembled inside, knowing this would lead to being hit on a bare behind with his belt. Distraught and terrified, I ran up the stairs to my bedroom vomiting from the fear of what would come next.

There was a theme of my father accusing me of crimes. Of course I had not committed any of them, but this gave him a reason to punish me. One Saturday afternoon, my father and his business partner were working on a project in the garage. I went out to ask my dad something. His business partner told me he had left to get something. I replied "Oh shucks." He interpreted this as "Oh Fuck," and when my father returned he was yelling and taking off his belt.

At the time I didn't even know the "F" word. It wasn't in my vocabulary and I wouldn't have said it to my father or his partner. I pleaded with my father that I did not say *that* word. "I didn't Daddy, I didn't, I swear I didn't, please Daddy." But he had already committed me to the crime. My mother was home and did what she did to intervene. So instead of the belt against my bare butt and legs, my mother washed my mouth out with soap.

It's now clear to me abusers are emotionally arrested and unable to process their own repressed anger and feelings of inadequacy. Instead, they take it out arbitrarily on their children or others they can exert power over. As for me, I tried desperately to please, to be a good girl so the wrath would not come crashing down on me. My attempts to please were to no avail. It is impossible to do the right thing when you are confronted with an angry child stuck in an adult body.

Another false accusation involved a piece of pie. To this day no one in our family has confessed to the crime. That a missing piece of pie would even be considered a crime demonstrates the hostility and need to control permeating my family environment. There was one piece of pie left and then there was none. My father, temper roaring, demanded to know who ate the last piece of pie. All of us were told to tattle on the guilty party or everyone would get a beating. Because I was the youngest of four girls, my sisters told me "Wendy, you confess, he won't hit you hard because you're the youngest." Wanting to please my older sisters, I confessed to eating the pie. I am certain his beating wasn't any less due to my age.

Because of incidents like these, I easily came to believe I was damaged and worth less than others. My sisters, for the most part, didn't want much to do with me, mostly (I assumed) because I wet the bed. As the youngest, my sisters saw me as the little spoiled brat. Having to sleep in the hallway because none of my sisters wanted me in their room confirmed for me I was insignificant.

The memories I did not have...the memories I buried for 30 years are the true story of my Fire. I share my true-life story with you because I want you to understand it is possible to heal from horrific and traumatic events and live life with joy and grace. I write this to you from the other side, unencumbered by others' stories and claims on me.

As it turns out, I was surrounded by abusers from birth through 12 years old. I was born into a tribe of perpetrators (male and female) who sexually, physically, and emotionally abused me. As is often the case, I was silenced by threats and actions of torture and death to my animals and loved ones.

My earliest memory of being scared is when I was in a crib as a toddler. My crib was in a bedroom with a window next to the stairwell leading to the second story of our two-flat home. The second story was rented out to two young men my parents allowed to babysit for me and my older sisters. I lay in my crib with soft blankets tucked around me and a little stuffed animal. The physical softness could not soothe my tense body. Peering through the slats in my crib, I could see the staircase from the upper flat through my window. I knew they were coming before the figures appeared. What stayed with me all these years is the feeling of the slight tremble of the crib as the young men pounded down the stairs. It would be the signal to me bad things were about to happen. Very bad things.

These young men terrorized and abused my sisters. They threatened them to assure they would never tell my parents. They held them hostage in a raging fire of abuse and fear which burned me as well. Witnessing the abuse of others energetically and emotionally abuses us as well.

I felt the fear of my sisters and heard their screams. On instinct, my adrenaline rose as my body heated up and curled into a fetal position, hoping somehow it would take me back to the safety of my mother's womb. Their hands may not have touched me, but I was burned by the energy of abuse they were inflicting upon my sisters. Hearing my sister's screams and feeling their terror forever altered the way my nervous system was wired. My flight or fight system was on constant alert.

A few years later, my father began slipping into my room at night while my sisters watched television. My mother often worked evenings as a waitress or a sales representative for various home party companies. While she was at work, my father was in charge. At first I welcomed the attention as any child starving for attention would. Then, when I was in kindergarten, I often spent the afternoons at my father's business shop, an electrical contract company. This was one of the ways he found to isolate me, and demand more. I lay as still as I could with nausea rising in my stomach from the familiar scent of Old Spice and sometimes alcohol. Every part of me wanted to scream, wanted him to go away. Since I could not leave him physically, my Spirit left my body. All sensations in my body ceased.

This was the start as my father prepared me for my induction into the larger group of pedophiles. The fondling led to rape and worse. It was my initiation into a dark sick world of pedophilia, a world two of my older sisters already knew too well.

This tribe included the supporting cast of women. When I told my paternal grandmother what my step-grandfather had done, she washed my genitals with bleach water. She thought this would make it right because somehow my vagina was to blame. I so desperately wanted her to protect me, to stop my grandfather, but as I quickly learned, I was on my own. I had no protectors. I had no one to stand up for me. The isolation and aloneness was as devastating as the abuse itself. My fear and feelings didn't matter. I didn't matter.

These women were more afraid of facing their own demons than protecting a child. They could never face the truth of what was happening to me because I suspect it happened to them. They buried their own stories and never allowed them to surface. Thus, they were unable to face the abuse being inflicted on my sisters and me.

2

The Gift of Fire

THE FIRE OF MY ABUSE was a training ground for my energy sensing abilities. Even as a toddler, I used my energy to feel the people near me. Who would be coming through the door? Was it the good daddy or the bad daddy? Would we go swimming or would I get a beating? Even the abuse was split...would he tell me he loved me as he slipped into the bedroom at night, that I was his beautiful little girl and he couldn't help himself, or would he threaten to kill my dog? To protect myself I learned at a very early age to sense which daddy was coming. Was it safe to be out and about? I could feel others' emotions. I knew if I needed to hide.

As I rose from the ashes and mended my fractures, I remembered I could communicate with animals and more. These gifts would be the beginning of my journey to understanding how I used my energy as a young child in an attempt to keep myself safe. I used my natural empathic abilities to read the people, animals, and situations around me.

We all come into the world sensing life around us through our personal energy field. Babies sense their world energetically, using the right side of their brain, until the adults around them begin encouraging them to learn language. As they learn language, they begin to use the left side of the brain more heavily, often resulting in less ability to sense energetically. Unlike most children who allow verbal language to become their primary form of communication, children burned by the fire of abuse and trauma hold onto their energy-sensing abilities to continually scan their environment. The need to stay aware of the energy and emotions of others exercises and builds their energy sensing abilities much like a workout does for muscles.

If you experienced physical, emotional, psychological, or sexual abuse or were parented by addicted or alcoholic parents, you too have experienced this Fire and its fractures. The Fire and the resulting fractures occur at many different levels. Being unwanted or emotionally abandoned can leave third degree burns and broken bits as much as physical, sexual, or ritual abuse. What is true for all of us is we can heal from the fire, mend our fractures, and take flight. When we heal, we can begin to find the intuitive gifts that arise from our healing. Like me, you can heal. Your experiences have gifted you with hyper-developed abilities to sense energy, and to connect and communicate with all life. You have been gifted with a deeper intuitive knowing and sensing. This is the gift of the Fractured Phoenix.

Along with this gift comes energetic sensitivity and fractured boundaries, which, when not managed properly, contribute and add to overwhelm, anxiety and depression, the last thing a trauma survivor needs. In this book I share with you how I learned to manage this sensitivity and show you how you too can take back your gifts, your power and your life. I will show you how to create a new myth from your story, the myth of the Fractured Phoenix.

3

The Visitation

The most horrendous weekend of my life was also my salvation. I was only four years old when my father took me and two of my sisters to a farm. I tried to run away from the barn where they kept us hostage. I tried to find the police and tell them what *they* were doing to my sisters and me. Surely the police would stop my father and his friends. But I never reached the police. My oldest sister was sent off to find and return me. She caught up with me as I tried to run through the ruts of the corn field. "You must come back", she said. "If you don't, it will be much worse for us all." Her words were as cold as my bare feet and nearly naked body on that late October day. My oldest sister was only nine years old herself. She had no choice but to return me.

She too knew what they were capable of doing. And to ensure I would not run away again, I was tied to a beam in the barn, in just my underwear. The ropes dug into my wrists as the straw on the floor poked into my shivering thighs.

Later, they strapped me to a cold, hard table. I felt I was facing death as my body shook from cold and fear. In retrospect, I don't think the adults had any intention of killing me, and given one of the perpetrators was a physician, I suspect they knew what they could do to terrorize me without leaving evidence of torture. Yet for me, death felt imminent. The pain I experienced as they used electrical shocks on my feet was to my four-year old self enough evidence death was upon me. I wished it so. I knew how to pray, "Dear God, please stop them. Please, God, please." But since God didn't stop them, my true essence left my body and was met by angelic beings in a world of unconditional love unlike anything I had ever known. I remember looking down on my body and those men. I remember the bright light from the filming equipment illuminating the horrific scene. I don't remember what my body felt. Thank God.

As horrible as the weekend was, I became aware of my connection with the Angelic beings. The fire and fractures would keep this hidden from my conscious mind for a few more decades, but deep in my being I knew. This remembrance gave me hope in times when hope was desperately needed. The Angelic beings allowed me to endure the next seven years until I was finally released from the torture of my abusers. The experience with the Angelic beings is how I was able to survive.

Other Fractured Phoenixes may have had similar experiences of sensing, seeing or hearing from a Divine Presence or Angelic beings. Some, like me, may have repressed the memory along with the terror. Still, there remains a sense of someone close yet unseen watching over us. These Angelic beings help us remember we are not alone. We are connected to a loving presence even when we have no evidence. We are not just our bodies. We are loving, spiritual beings experiencing life in human form.

4

The Animal Helpers

MY HEALING AND RISE from the ashes was aided by the animals from my childhood. They helped me stay sane. A review of childhood photos reveals how I clung to them and tried to guard them. This need to guard was because any misdeeds or attempts to tell about the abuse often resulted in threats, harm, or death to animals I cared about. Unfortunately, this is not unusual. Using animals to keep children quiet is a common pedophile strategy.

Like many young girls, I had an obsession with horses. My first ride on a horse was with my mother when I was about four years old. We lived in a rented farmhouse just outside the city where the farmer had a few horses. I don't remember much from then, but I suspect that first ride was where my obsession began.

When I was 10 ½ my dreams finally came true. My sister and I were given a horse. He was originally given to my stepfather's daughter but because she was afraid of the horse, he was given to us. Walker was a tall, buckskin colored quarter horse-thoroughbred cross who was green broke. This meant he hadn't been completely started under saddle nor ridden much.

During our first summer with Walker, Mom would drop us off in the morning at the stables and pick us up late in the day. We were given a little bit of guidance from the stable manager but otherwise we were on our own. Walker bucked us off repeatedly and each time we climbed back on. Fortunately, we only suffered bruises. We learned to ride the buck and stay in the saddle or on his bare back. Eventually, he became a very trustworthy horse. We trained him to rear on command, not something I advise you to do. We rode him all over the streets of Madison's west side, fed him root beer and let him drink out of water fountains at the park. We galloped on him bareback either riding double or borrowing another horse from the stable to venture off on a quest. At the time I didn't realize how important these days of freedom would be to my well being as an adult. Being able to connect with this magnificent animal and the sense of power and freedom while riding buffered my psyche from the abuse which was happening at home. This would bond me to horses in a way I wouldn't truly appreciate until decades later.

When we moved to a farm 20 minutes outside of Madison, Mom bought us a pony to go with our horse. Tony the pony was a handful. My sister and I often went off on adventures with Walker and Tony. By then, no amount of bucking, twisting or trying to rub us off on trees worked for our pony. We had acquired good "seats" and could ride most anything. A few years later we became more interested in school and boys and Walker and Tony were sold.

5

The Energy Connection

WHEN I WAS NINE YEARS OLD, my parents divorced. I remember my father gathering my sisters and me together as he sat in his living room chair. With tears in his eyes, he told us "Mommy doesn't love Daddy anymore." "I don't want to leave you, but Mommy doesn't want me to live here anymore." He left out the part about him cheating on her (and not discreetly) then coming home from deer hunting with crabs instead of a deer. My mother was devastated by his cheating and wasn't willing to put up with it anymore. She wouldn't tell me about his indiscretions until many years later.

And consistent with Stockholm syndrome, where captives begin to side with and attach to their captors, I was devastated that my father was leaving. It may seem odd, but he gave me attention and the horrible things he had done to me and allowed to be done to me had already been erased from my conscious memory. It's also possible the pedophile ring had used hypnotism and brainwashing on me to keep me attached to my father.

Because I had been using my energy to sense others, I felt my mother's grief and anger. I felt my father's depression and shame. I felt my sister's grief and confusion. I felt everyone's feelings. I became the voice of it all. I cried for everyone. I screamed for everyone. I had become good at feeling everyone and took it all on. Because I didn't know why my mother was kicking my father out, I blamed her for all I was feeling. I had no idea how to process the entire family's grief at nine years old. All I knew how to do was cry, scream, and cry some more. I became labeled as very sensitive, and not in a good way.

The energy sensing and empathic abilities we use to keep us safe eventually create problems. Because we do this unconsciously, we are unaware that we are sending our personal energy out, while picking up and taking on the energy of others, and fracturing our energy boundaries. We have no concept of our energy body.

We are too young and uninformed to know that the Universe is pure energy. Every thing, every planet, every person, every animal and plant is energy. What we refer to as Spirits are also energy, but of a different vibration. All of this is connected in a network or grid of energy. Nothing is separate. We are like a drop of water in an ocean. Taken out of the ocean, we appear separate, but as part of the ocean, we cannot identify a "separate" us. When we are in a physical body we are the drop; when we leave our physical body we go back to the ocean although we still have awareness of our "drop."

This understanding of energy is the cornerstone of ancient Eastern philosophies, and recently from the field of science known as quantum mechanics or quantum physics.

Energy is known as Qi or Chi, in acupuncture, eastern martial arts, Qigong, or Reiki and considered the life force.

In quantum physics, scientists have discovered that matter may appear solid, but it is actually vibrating energy, a never-ending movement of light particles and waves that create form. Scientists have observed that no matter what substance they analyze, it all comes down to one basic substance from which All originates.

I acknowledge this is a simplistic explanation of a pioneering field of science. It's not my intention to provide you with all of the supporting science for my understanding of how energy works. Others have done this already. One who has done it quite well is

Lynn McTaggert in her book, *The Field*. As she shares in the prologue, *"At our most elemental, we are not a chemical reaction, but an energetic charge. Human beings and all living things are a coalescence of energy in a field of energy connected to every other thing in the world. This pulsating energy field is the central engine of our being and consciousness, the alpha and the omega of our existence."* To understand this at a deeper level, I recommend that you read her book.

This all-encompassing energy is often referred to symbolically as God, Source, Great Spirit, Love, Divine Essence, or the Great Mystery, and is the basis of everything solid, liquid, gas, or ethereal. Every person, plant, or animal originates from it. We may look different, but all originate from the same source. We are only different in composition and vibration and we are all connected. There is no "distance" between anything through this connection.

Our energy body or personal energy field is a multilayered electromagnetic field. It is the first place we meet the world. Known as our auric field, it typically extends about 2-3 feet out from our body in a cocoon-like dimension. It extends above and below the body as well.

For those of us who have experienced the fire and fractures of a broken childhood, our auric field often extends out further than others. As our energy field touches others, we often sense or take on the other's energy. Our auric field is more permeable or sensitive than other people who have not used their energy early on to "read" others.

Normally, our auric field would have more definitive boundaries, making us less sensitive to other's energy. Because of the different forms of abuse, our energy boundaries where "invaded" by others. This frequent intrusion of boundaries weakens them. Additionally, our frequent need to "read" other people caused us to weaken these boundaries as well. This is how we end up feeling other people's emotional and physical states. Learning how to manage your personal energy field and its boundaries is crucial to healing your fractures and embracing your intuitive gifts. I share more later in the book to guide you.

6

The Last Flames & Fractures

SHORTLY AFTER THE DIVORCE, my mother met a man who would become my first stepfather. He had lots of "class" but wasn't especially fond of children. He built us a nice w house across the street from where we lived. He s the one who gave us Walker, the horse. He bought only sweet dog for our family named Lucky. Lucky, B any Spaniel, had very impressive breeding. His par and grandparents were all champion bird trial dogky didn't carry these genes; he was terrified of te never lived up to my stepfather's expectati I loved him dearly. Like my dog Duchess, he used to keep me quiet. He didn't have to sac fe for it since I already knew I mustn't tell t my stepfather was doing to me.

My stepfather liked to drink, a lot. Every night around 5:30 pm was cocktail hour. When he drank excessively, he became violent. The first time we witnessed this he went after my mother and began hitting her. Terrified, my sister called the police. Hopeful he would be gone, I was soon disappointed. As I stood at the top of the stairs, I heard my mother say "It's okay officers; we're fine. We just had a little too much to drink." My heart sank. Okay? How could she possibly think this was okay?

The next time it happened, he went after one of my sisters. This was different. My mother went after him and left trails of blood down his back where she clawed him. I tried calling the police, but he ripped the phone out of my hands pulling the cord out of the wall and threw it across the kitchen. When his attention left me, I was in survival mode and dashed to my bedroom where I had my own phone and called the police. This time my mother sent him to jail. She divorced him shortly thereafter and we moved to a farm outside the city. I was 12 years old and with my father and stepfather out of my life, the abuse finally stopped.

However, even though the abuse had stopped, I was not yet out of the fire. The repressed memories of my abuse lay dormant in my psyche. A part of us always remembers while another part continues to repress. My survival depended on keeping those memories locked away from my consciousness so I could function in the world. The truth of what happened was much too horrible to bear. To keep the memories down, I used drugs and alcohol.

In the late sixties and early seventies it was not difficult to find recreational drugs, even for a 13 year old. My school was full of them. Even before 13, I had access to alcohol and learned from the adults around me that when you don't want to feel, alcohol is the ticket to numbness. I followed adults around at many cocktail parties, picking up their half empty glasses to finish them off. The numbness that followed allowed my adrenaline-filled body to relax, if only for a short time.

When I reached high school, I was influenced by friends who got high on marijuana. With a boyfriend as a dealer, I always had access to weed, but it never did anything except make me paranoid and hungry so I never used it past the first few times. Speed (amphetamines – diet pills), was my drug of choice and easy to pick up in the halls of Madison West High School. With a little tablet of White Cross, I could feel invincible. I could go days without eating more than a few bites of food here and there. This would help me feel slim and attractive as well. Of course, when I came down off the White Cross, my emotions crashed as well. It was easy to solve the ensuing emotional crash by raiding my mother's liquor cabinet. Vodka, which was her drink of choice, made it easy for me to steal my share without suspicion from her by watering it down.

We live in a society that encourages us to drown our feelings with alcohol, food, and prescribed medications. "It's Miller time," time to ignore that voice inside of you that is desperately trying to get your attention. We stuff down our anger with chocolate and release our tension with alcohol. We ignore the whispers of our intuition until they become shouts that turn into illness or messed up situations. We medicate with anti-anxiety meds until we no longer know what we truly want or need in our lives. We become numb to our own inner knowing and to our emotional self. It's no wonder then that those of us with horrendous memories often turn to alcohol, drugs, and food for numbing and comfort. We reach for what is easily accessible.

Once in college, I relied on amphetamines (aka Speed or White Cross) to keep me focused on my work. Alcohol was completely acceptable in college, so I continued to use it to numb my feelings as well. I wasn't aware of what I was stuffing. The memories never surfaced during this time. I needed to stuff the self-image and shame I adopted as a result of the abuse, and the pain of believing I was so much less than everyone else. I didn't understand why I felt this way. I didn't remember anyone telling me I was a piece of shit and yet, I believed I was worthless. This was my most debilitating fracture. I felt unlovable and unwanted. It was the belief born out of the suppressed reality that my life meant so little to my father that he would share me with his pedophile friends who tortured me. But the actual memory of those events was hidden deep in the embers of the fire.

Eventually, the Speed affected my relationship with my boyfriend, and at his insistence, I flushed the remainders of my recent White Cross purchase down the toilet, never to pop another again. I wouldn't give up the alcohol for another two decades.

Abusing alcohol, amphetamines, and prescription drugs for pain heaped on top of my repressed memories created bouts of deep depression. The anti-depressants I was given made it much worse (which we now understand happens with young adults). At 17 (my first year of college), I slipped so far into the black hole of depression I almost didn't make it. I almost checked out. As I lay sobbing on my bed in my apartment, I decided it just wasn't worth it anymore. I had a full bottle of antidepressants and a full bottle of Percodan (a narcotic prescribed to me for cramps). I grabbed a glass of water and stuffed them all in. And that would have been the end, except some part of me wasn't ready to leave. Perhaps it was the part of me that knew I was loved from my out-of-body experience.

I picked up the phone to call my mother and say goodbye. I didn't tell her what I had taken but her instincts understood. As I lay vomiting on the floor of the basement, the police and paramedics broke in.

When I woke up in the ICU the next day, I was surrounded by my sisters and my mother. They were devastated. They really did love me, and then I realized I had almost done the most selfish thing possible. At that moment, I knew no matter how bad I felt, suicide was not the way out. I would need to find a different way to bring light into my life.

My suicide attempt was the ultimate act of numbing and was a turning point for me. Something happened to me that day in the ICU unit. With the realization I couldn't leave this world without inflicting great pain on others, I decided to *find a way* to make my life better. Somewhere inside I made a decision to find a way. I would find a way to understand the deep pain that lived inside me. I would find a way to lift myself out of the black hole that had surrounded me for so long. I would find a way to heal my fractures. I knew I needed help. I knew I needed a different therapist. It would take me a decade to find her.

In the meantime, I needed to feel worthy. I believed if I could contribute something to the world, if I could "save others," I would be okay. I felt a yearning to lead others. Surely if others looked to me as a leader, I must be okay. Following my mother's footsteps in business and marketing, I became involved with a student organization for marketing. I found something I was good at and a group I felt I belonged to. I picked myself up and over the next few years became a national officer in the Junior Collegiate division of the Distributive Education Clubs of America, and graduated with honors from the University of Wisconsin.

I collected awards and honors like knick-knacks. The Chancellors' Award, Young Achievers Award, Marketer of the Year Award, Exemplary Education Service Award for Economic Development, Cum Laude Honors, Special Service Award, and more. And still, I often felt less than. I still often felt as if I were broken. I had still not recalled the memories of my childhood, but the damage on my psyche from the betrayal was not hidden. Even though the fire had been extinguished, the burning embers still clung to me, singeing the flesh of my self esteem. The fractures made it difficult for me to walk in the world and feel normal.

But the belief that I was less than, broken or damaged goods, was a lie. I was not broken, and never had been. Neither are you broken. Our abusive and/or neglectful treatment as children led us to believe we are not worthy of kindness or love. We create false beliefs about our value as humans. We make up stories about how we must be bad, defective, or unworthy to have caused those who should love us to treat us so badly. We internalized the abuse as our fault. We blame and shame ourselves for not being more lovable.

All of this is bullshit. It is the coping mechanism of a child's brain trying to sort out the unfathomable. A child does not have the capacity to understand she is being manipulated. That she is being told lies about her inherent loveliness. But in order to counteract the beliefs constructed by your child self, you must begin to listen to her. You must begin a conversation with your young self to hear her and help her understand where her beliefs are wrong.

7

The Healing Begins

THOUGH I DATED MANY MEN and even married one for a year, only one would have the gentleness I needed to trust others again. Technically my second husband, but in my mind, my only husband, Steve became the stability and safety I needed to begin to heal. With him I felt safe for the first time in my life. I remember so clearly on our first date as we drove to the movie theater how I felt as if we had been together for years. There was no need to be anyone but myself. I knew I would be safe with him, and knew right then we would eventually marry.

When we married three years later, my childhood memories were still repressed. Though I had always looked inward to understand why I felt and behaved as I did, this crucial piece was still elusive.

Unfortunately the sexual dysfunction from the abuse became apparent on the honeymoon. I went from being passionate and willing to avoiding making love almost overnight. I didn't understand what was wrong with me and decided if I drank, I could get through it. And so I drank whenever the possibility of making love came up. The shame and guilt of not being the perfect wife eroded my fragile sense of self-worth. How could he love me like this? I wasn't worthy of being loved. I was clueless about why I felt this way, and there was too much shame to talk about it with him or anyone else.

How do you tell someone you love, admire, find attractive and enjoy being with that you are terrified of making love with them? It made no sense to me except to conclude that somehow I was defective. Seriously damaged. Seriously fucked up.

During our third year of marriage, I encountered an abusive boss at my work which was the catalyst to finding the therapist I would trust enough to allow my memories to come forth. She was God-sent and I was ready. My hour with her was a sanctuary, and felt like a warm down comforter on a cold winter's night. She welcomed and accepted me unconditionally with a compassion I had never experienced. The trust I felt with her allowed the memories to surface. She helped me to see it wasn't my fault. I hadn't done anything wrong. I wasn't a burden. Through her eyes, I began to see the incredibly brave little girl who lived inside of me.

As part of my early therapy I began "listening within." It was simple in some ways, perhaps because the memories were desperate to surface. As I sat in my therapist's office, I would get quiet and listen for the feelings and memories to come forth without any prompting or suggestion from her. Because I trusted my therapist so completely, I was able to share most of what I heard. It was difficult for these memories to surface when I wasn't in the safety of her office.

There was no rhyme or reason to how the memories came forth. Vignettes of people and places flooded my inner eye, accompanied by visceral physical reactions which took over my body. Often, I trembled, shook, screamed and nearly vomited from what I was experiencing. Only my therapist's voice, gently guiding me back to the present, kept me from completely living the flashback. Other times, something in the outside world, like a deer dead on the side of the road, would send me spinning backward in time. My well developed sense of dissociation helped me cope until I could get to a safe place.

There was a particular memory which continued to haunt me, often triggered by animals dead on the side of the road. To cope with these flashbacks, I used a process known as Eye Movement Desensitization and Reprocessing or EMDR. By focusing on the memory while following a target to move my eyes from left to right, I was able to disconnect the emotional re-action to the memory from the flashbacks. Thus, the flashbacks no longer had the emotional charge. It was my group therapist who helped me with EMDR. As part of the process, my therapist asked me to imagine someone coming to rescue me, someone who could stop the "bad people." Because of the brainwashing I had endured, the small child inside of me could not imagine anyone, not even God, who could stop them. Eventually, we were able to convince the small child that they indeed could be stopped, and of course, the rescue involved horses.

I listened to those small parts of me who were scared, angry, and some silent, but for the pictures they drew. I didn't have an "inner child," I had "inner children" ... plural. There were 11 distinctive voices and personalities that arose in my inner world. I honored each one by giving them a special colored pen to write with. I let them tell me their names, their ages, and allowed them to express whatever they needed me to hear. Some of them were very young and could only cry or scribble. Some of them drew pictures of "what the doctor did to them"... knowing that this was an abuser, not a caring doctor.

Some of them were very angry and wanted to torture, dismember and kill their abusers. It was hard to blame them. Some of them carried enormous grief from having witnessed the torture and death of animals they loved.

To help them feel safe, I took a very large piece of poster board and drew boxes in it, like rooms in a house. Each child had their own room which I "decorated" with pictures from a catalog of children's linens. This became their safe house. When memories or outside circumstances became overwhelming, they could go to their safe house.

The power of listening within, and giving voice to these parts of me was remarkable. At the time I first started listening, I was suffering with gastric ulcers, fibromyalgia and chronic fatigue. Often I would go into a therapy session with severe stomach pain that would be relieved as I listened within. The more I listened and nurtured those inner children, the healthier I became. My ulcers vanished. My fibromyalgia and chronic fatigue symptoms lessened and disappeared except for times of great stress.

When you begin to listen in, you must do so without judgment. Whatever needs to be expressed by your young self (selves) needs to be allowed complete acceptance and unconditional love. You will need to become the loving parent you never had. You can re-parent yourself. You can allow the young parts to express their pain, their anger, their guilt and their grief. This young part of you carries an energy that was never allowed to be expressed. To heal the fractures, this energy needs to be set free. If it is not, it will manifest as illness.

This will not be easy. Listening within has been the most difficult part of healing my fractures. It takes a tremendous amount of courage to allow those suffering parts a place in your life and yet you must. They need a voice. The crying and screams they suppressed are still wailing inside you, reverberating as a discordant energy that unattended will become disease. Time will never heal these fractures but self-love and compassion will, and provide you wings to soar.

Being faced with these memories shattered my world in many ways. I had constructed an entire childhood based on bits and pieces of happy memories while obliterating the difficult reality of the abuse. It felt as if the earth had opened up and I was falling down a hole with no end. I didn't want to believe what I was hearing and feeling, yet the reality of the visions, the extreme terror and visceral emotion that accompanied the memories couldn't be denied. I would have given anything for these memories to not be true, for my constructed childhood to be the truth. I wanted to think of my childhood as normal and fun. But what I had created in my mind of my childhood was but a child's fantasy. The true documentary was a horror film I could barely fathom.

Over the next seven years, the stability of my marriage, my awesome therapists, and my willingness to listen within compassionately allowed me to mend my fractures. I don't know if I would have been able to do the deep work without the love and gentleness of my husband. To face such horrible truths required me to cut off any communication with my father, and for a time, my mother as well. My father was in my life only on holidays and we had no relationship, so cutting him off was simple. Extricating me from family Christmas gatherings and other events was much more difficult. My mother and I were very close. I looked up to her and admired her on so many levels. We did many things together. Yet, I knew in order to truly heal, I would need to separate myself from her, at least for awhile. I did this because she couldn't bring herself to believe my father had done the things both I and my older sister were remembering. I couldn't have her doubt in my life when my own sense of believing what I was remembering was so very fragile. Having Steve by my side made this possible.

As much as Steve tried to be supportive, he was not equipped to provide the level of support I needed. Many of us rising from the ashes find this to be true-- the heat of the fire is too much for others to bear. They tend to step back from the flames as we rise up, as our childhood and false self are burned from our being.

As part of my therapy, love making was off the table unless I initiated it. Now that I understood why making love was so difficult, I expected to be able to let go of the guilt and shame. Still, I felt terribly guilty. I tried to make up for it by being the perfect wife in every other way. A part of me was desperate to be good enough without being sexual, but my early life training set me up to fail. Deep inside I believed my worth was dependent upon being able to please a man sexually. It was how I seemed to garner my father's love, and how I was able to attract many men as a young woman.

I was convinced that if I couldn't be sexual, I had no worth.

It was hard for me to understand why Steve wanted to stay married to me. How could he love me? He didn't sign up for this. He met a woman who was fun, who wanted a thriving career, loved to travel with him, and was carefree. The woman he married turned into a scared child, unable to make love or even work full-time. And still, he stood by me as best he could.

Although his best was good, like so many others trapped in the nest with the rising Fractured Phoenix, the transformation and flight can leave them bewildered. As I healed my fractures and reclaimed my true self, the new Phoenix that emerged was not the one he had married. Subtle differences began to emerge in our relationship. My search for a spiritual connection would grow in importance to me. Because of his strict religious upbringing, he avoided anything that even hinted of organized religion as if it was a deadly disease. I appeased myself by thinking it wasn't important. As long as we loved each other it would be okay. As I began to avoid alcohol, I found it difficult to go out with our friends when everyone ended up drunk. I now understood drinking to this excess was about avoiding feelings and being numb to an inner life. This understanding only seemed to drive a deeper divide between us. I desperately needed emotional intimacy, and he was not equipped to provide what I craved.

Steve was an example of how those around a rising Fractured Phoenix often respond. They are not experiencing the same transformation and are likely not to as they have not been in the fire. I imagine it feels like a betrayal to them when the person they love transforms into a new person with different desires, beliefs, and needs. And because very rarely do any of us survive childhood without some self esteem issues, I suspect he too had fractures.

8

Stepping Onto the Spiritual Path

COMFORT AND SECURITY can become a trap that stunts our Soul growth. Sometimes, you have to leave everything behind, take a leap even when it is terrifying, and walk into the unknown (which is where I found myself 18 years later after 15 years of marriage). I did not want to see that we had grown so far apart. While I had changed, he was still the same guy. Nothing wrong with that; he was his authentic self. Me, I wanted more from my life: more depth, more connection to Spirit, more understanding of the world, more connection to friends, and more animals in my life.

After seven years of individual therapy and three years of group therapy, a different woman emerged. The Phoenix began to rise. The turning point came when I read *A Return to Love* by Marianne Williamson on a plane ride from the west coast. Her book had such a profound effect on me, that I typed up three pages of quotes to sustain me in my day-to-day world. I kept them in my briefcase and referred to them often (I still keep the same tattered pages in my night stand). Whenever fear would begin to seep in, I took out the paper and read. Quotes like the following, were instrumental in healing my thought process.

Love is what we were born with. Fear is what we have learned here. The spiritual journey is the unlearning of fear and the acceptance of love back into our hearts. Love is the essential existential fact. It is our ultimate reality and our purpose on earth. To be consciously aware of it, to experience love in ourselves and in others, is the meaning of life.

The change we are looking for is inside our hearts. The ups and downs in life are always going to happen; they are part of the human experience. What we can change, however, is how we perceive them. And that shift in our perception is a miracle.

God is the love within us. Whether we "follow" Him or think with love is entirely up to us. When we choose to love, or to allow our minds to be one with God, then life is peaceful. When we turn away from love, the pain sets in. And whether we love, or close our hearts to love, is a mental choice we make every moment of every day.

These quotes from *A Return to Love,* helped me remember what was truly important in life. They reminded me I always had a choice as to how I could interpret what was happening in my life. Marianne Williamson also wrote extensively in this book about forgiveness.

Forgiveness. Yes, I could forgive my father when I could see him in my mind as a wounded child acting out. He never had the opportunity to heal and so he repeated the abuse he had suffered. Because I had spent seven years feeling much of the anger and betrayal, I was able to forgive. I wasn't using the idea of forgiveness to avoid feeling the pain of the abuse, but it was a powerful catalyst to my healing.

The woman who emerged after seven years of processing wasn't bitter and she wasn't a victim. She was a survivor intent on healing. Her heart was just beginning to break open and it was the beginning of the end of her marriage.

What followed for me was a journey into the discovery of who I really am. It included reading Gary Zukav, Wayne Dyer, Marianne Williamson, *A Course in Miracles,* and every other book I could find that would help me make sense of the world and my feelings. As I began to understand that we create our own reality, that is, we create the meaning of what happens in our life, I realized, I could create new meaning. I didn't need to see myself as a victim. I could see a larger vision of my life experiences. I decided to make a positive meaning of what happened to me.

I read about Soul contracts. This is the idea that each of us as Souls before coming to this life chooses who we interact with in this world, and we chose the essence of what we experience. It occurred to me that perhaps my Soul chose this early childhood experience. Whether this was true or not didn't matter. It gave me a sense of power. Though I couldn't change what happened to me, I could change how I responded. This helped tremendously in my healing. Though I caution, you cannot jump to this point without first digging up the anger, fear and shame that accompanies the memories. It all needs to come up and be processed before you can move forward. And if you never choose to hold the idea of Soul contracts, that is completely okay. We each get to choose what we make of our experiences.

As I became more aware of my true desires, my work evolved out of advertising into academia and then finally self-employment. All part of a plan I hadn't consciously initiated, but which was being directed by my higher self.

From my readings, I began to understand we are all energy beings. The idea that we are all energy beings connected by energy made sense to me because of my out-of-body experiences as a young child. I knew of the dimensions beyond this physical world. I had been there. The idea of Spirits made complete sense to me. While out of my body, I felt as one with the Angelic beings. While I didn't have the vocabulary as a young child to express how energy works, I understood it on a deep, personal level. The books merely described what I had already experienced.

The abusive boss, who triggered the buried memories, gave me another gift. Each morning before going to work, I would spend 30 minutes meditating. I first learned to meditate at 17 when I took a transcendental meditation class. I had never developed a regular practice until I was compelled to in order to deal with the abusive boss.

Throughout my "recovery" and beyond, I would spend time in the stillness. It was in this stillness where I was able to notice the pain and suffering I had buried. In the quiet, I could listen without judgment and give space for my feelings to emerge. Many years later, I discovered two books by Pete Walker which were instrumental in helping me love, accept, and understand my shame and pain. I highly recommend his books, *Complex PTSD* and *The Tao of Fully Feeling.* Every adult child of abuse can benefit from these books. The books helped me see how subtle the shame can be; it helped me identify when my shame was being triggered so I could confront and release it.

After you have had an opportunity to process your memories with a professional, I urge you to consider developing your own meditation practice. When we are able to sit with ourselves, our pain, and feelings, we can begin to soften our hearts towards ourselves. It's challenging for us to sit in the silence because often there are parts of us screaming to be heard and it's easier to quiet them with busyness. Start very slowly. Five minutes is enough. Then as you develop a daily practice of five minutes you can begin to increase the time. The daily practice is the most important aspect in the beginning. Eventually, you will crave your time in the stillness. You will find your life flows more easily and external circumstances are less disruptive.

However, if at any time during your practice you find yourself experiencing intrusive thoughts, hyper-ventilating, or other signs of flashbacks, stop and seek help from a trauma professional. Though this isn't common, it does happen for some people.

9

Healing the Body

As I PROCESSED THE REPRESSED MEMORIES of my childhood, it became evident the experiences were not only trapped in my mind, but also trapped energetically in my body. Constant pain in my neck and back led me to a rheumatologist who diagnosed me with fibromyalgia. The treatment was antidepressants. The drug worked for the pain. Unfortunately, it also made me so drowsy I couldn't get out of bed to go to work. When I went off the drug, I was in pain and needed relief. I was led to a healer through my horses.

Once a physical therapist for people, Carrie and her partner were now helping horses. Soon Carrie would choose to go back to working with people, not in the clinical setting she once worked but on her own, where she blended physical therapy, cranial sacral therapy, and a variety of energy healing modalities. She was pivotal in my understanding of how my abuse affected me physically and energetically. I learned the memories were literally trapped in my body. Often sessions would result in memories surfacing and releasing with tears. Through the physical therapy and energy work, I was able to heal a great deal of the trauma buried in my body.

About the same time, another healer came into my life and I began weekly yoga and bi-weekly energy work with her. One week I was with one healer, and the next week with another. This, combined with weekly group therapy and weekly individual therapy, allowed me to move forward through the memories. I became stronger physically and emotionally. I faced the difficult memories and learned to comfort the scared parts of myself. Being compassionate with myself, and nurturing and mothering the little parts of me inside was never easy. Of all I have learned, loving and being compassionate with myself has been the most healing for me.

If you have experienced chronic fatigue, chronic pain, fibromyalgia, autoimmune disease or weight gain, it's likely related to your early childhood experiences. Through a groundbreaking study, we now understand there is a correlation between early childhood trauma and disease. The Adverse Childhood Experiences

(ACE) study was conducted by the Kaiser Permanente (an HMO in California) and the Center for Disease Control and Prevention. Participants were recruited during 1995-97 and then studied long term for health outcomes. The study has shown a clear correlation between adverse childhood experiences (physical, emotional or sexual abuse, alcoholic or drug addicted parent, death of parent or sibling, debilitating disease, etc.) and health and social problems as adults. Results suggest varying forms of abuse or family dysfunction in childhood contribute significantly to health problems decades later. Included are chronic diseases such as cancer, stroke, heart disease, autoimmune disorders, obesity and diabetes type 2. The higher the ACE "score," meaning the more adverse experiences, the more likely a person is to have one or more of the aforementioned diseases.

Since the early 70s, Peter Levine has done extensive work understanding the relationship between early trauma and the long term effects on our flight or fight system. When a child is traumatized, his or her natural flight or fight system becomes stuck in the "on" position. With this system over activated, small events can trigger a flood of hormones, which cause inflammation in the body. Over time, this repetitive inflammation creates disease. Unless a person is guided to "shut off" this system, inflammation, anxiety, depression and panic attacks can result.

Trauma affects the body in other ways as well. It may surprise you to learn our bodies provide us more information than our minds. Our bodies and our senses inform our minds, which creates what we believe about the world. Raised in a safe, loving home without severe illness or trauma, children learn to trust what they experience physically in their world. They experiment with touch and movement and integrate sight and sound to learn. They are embodied.

A child who experiences pain, terror, or physical trauma grows up believing the world is unsafe, and more importantly, their body is a vehicle for pain and anxiety. They learn to avoid physical sensations by dissociating from their bodies. By dissociating, they not only escape physical and emotional pain, they also leave behind the rich wisdom available through bodily sensations. When this dissociation continues into adulthood, anxiety, depression, repressed rage, and anger eat away at their emotional and physical well being. Until we consciously come back into our body and learn to decipher the messages of our bodies, we will be blocked in our healing. Learning body awareness is essential in healing the fractures.

Fortunately, there are many healing modalities to address the overactive flight or fight system, create body awareness, and reverse the process. Peter Levine's work has resulted in a technique known as Somatic Experience which addresses both blocked energy and body awareness. Other modalities include Bodytalk, Heller work, The Emotion Code, Emotional Freedom Technique (EFT or Tapping) and others (more information in Chapter 34). In one way or another, they address finding the areas in the body where energy has been blocked or trapped from a physical or emotional trauma, and releasing the block so energy can flow again. Some also address body awareness. In turn, the flight or fight system is quieted and can return to normal. This type of healing is critical for the Fractured Phoenix to mend the broken places. Without this, trauma festers in the body, causing physical and emotional pain.

As the Fractured Phoenix rises from the ashes, healing on all levels (body, energy, emotional, spiritual, mental-mindset) needs to occur. Fractures require time to heal and often heal in layers. As one layer of healing occurs, another is eventually revealed. It's like peeling an onion. Time between the layers allows integration and alignment. There is no need to rush your healing. Allow yourself time and be gentle with yourself.

10

Finding My Spiritual Home

ONE OF MY ENERGY HEALERS often spoke of going to church. I was curious what kind of church this "new-age" woman would be so engaged in. This was when I discovered Unity. Unity was not formed as a church, but as an educational organization based on Christianity. However, this form of Christianity embraced all other beliefs and paths, knowing that all led to the same omnipotent loving presence more commonly referred to as God.

As I sat in the pew on my first visit, I was struck by the genuine love and acceptance I could sense from the people surrounding me. The "sermon" was uplifting and loving. We were guided into a meditation and a period of silence supported by beautiful piano music.

I could feel my heart opening, my energy expanding and an opening to Spirit. The energy in the room was filling me with love. Yes, this. This was what I was searching for. It was a community open to love and acceptance of all people. As the service closed, everyone stood forming a circle and holding hands singing *Let there be Peace on Earth*. Tears formed in my eyes and rolled down my cheeks as I sang from the depths of my being. This song, this was my song. *Let There Be Peace on Earth* was the song I chose for my wedding to Steve. I had found my way home.

Having found a spiritual home at Unity, my search for a closer understanding of God/Source would create a wedge between Steve and me. Here was a community of people who understood how it felt to be connected to Spirit. There was no judgment or criticism of those who believed differently, just a genuine desire to be a conduit of love in the world. I became a member of Unity, attending each service alone. I tried to help Steve understand this was not like the strict Lutheran church he was raised in, but he could not bring himself to step inside the doors. Literally.

Once I was responsible for taking photographs of an event for the newsletter but found the batteries in my camera were dead. I called Steve who generously agreed to bring them the 20 mile distance to me. When he arrived, I needed to go outside to the car to get the batteries as he would not step inside the "church." My heart was deeply saddened that we could not share this journey. I wanted him to experience the love and acceptance I felt with this understanding of our world.

As much as I pleaded, he resisted. Eventually I decided it wasn't important. He was caring and loving which should be enough for me. I didn't realize it wasn't enough. I didn't realize how desperately I needed emotional and spiritual intimacy. I was telling myself a lie so I could continue our relationship. Eventually the lie and buried feelings would rise just as I, the Fractured Phoenix, was rising. The heat would extinguish our marriage.

11

Discovering the Gifts

As the fire began to burn off the false self I had developed over the years to cope and fit in, I began to discern what was important to me. I remembered my love for horses and realized I could bring them back into my life. This led me to remember my ability to hear the animals. As a child, animals were my confidantes. They were the only beings I trusted. I heard them when I was little. I remember telling my mother one day how our kitty had a tummy ache. She looked at me and said with a sigh, "Wendy, don't make up stories. You don't know how the kitty feels." And so I stopped telling others what I heard, and eventually, buried those memories with the others.

Now, as I paid attention to what was important to

me, I bought a horse and stabled him down the road. Smokey, a black Tennessee Walking Horse, was a gentle, steady Soul. He spent the first six years of his life in the horrific Big Lick show circuit of Tennessee. The high stepping action seen in the Big Lick show circuit for Tennessee Walking horses is not a natural movement. It's an exaggerated movement caused by creating pain to the horse's legs. Trainers will put a caustic material on the horse's front legs which causes burning. Then, they put chains on the legs to irritate the already sore leg causing the horse to jerk his hooves up as he moves. This is known as "soring." Smokey's front legs had scars delineated with white hair from the "soring" he was forced to endure. When he came into my life, I promised him he would never be shown again and never hurt or mistreated. We had an instant connection, in part because we shared an abusive past. Over the years, I've observed from my work how people are drawn to animals that mirror their own wounds. A woman abandoned by her mother connects with a foal rejected by its mother. She understands the pain of this abandonment and by comforting the foal, she also comforts herself. The shared experiences create an emotional resonance between them.

Though Smokey was a gentle Soul and very trustworthy, he was also shut down. The years of hurtful humans had taught him to do whatever was asked without disagreement to avoid pain. It was also without joy. We both had shut down after years of abuse. We chose compliance over the risk of pain. Our common wounds allowed us to bond and understand each other and eventually, we both found joy again together.

Once in the beginning of our relationship, I used a lunge whip to ask him to move forward while working with him in the arena. I could tell by the terror in his eyes that whips meant pain. Perhaps this was the origin of the scar across his face. Though I never would have hit him with the whip, I understood the fear an object can create, and never used a whip with him again. I discovered all I needed to do was ask for the walk, gait, or canter, and he would follow my verbal instructions.

The first time I rode him in the indoor arena, he followed my commands by following my thoughts. I was amazed when I realized all I needed to do was think about where I wanted to go and he would head there. As much as we understood each other, I still hadn't remembered my ability to communicate with the animals.

A couple years after Smokey came into my life, the stable owner announced an animal communicator was coming to our barn to give a presentation and do "readings." At the time, I was skeptical but curious. I listened to her talk about her experience, and when my turn for the reading came, we walked out to Smokey's paddock where she began to communicate with him. Though I was unsure of this animal communication thing, I often sent thoughts and pictures to Smokey about what was happening in our lives. I didn't think about this consciously; it just seemed a natural thing to do. The animal communicator began describing Smokey's personality. She was accurate, yet I remember thinking, "She could have guessed this." Then she told me, "He wants to know when you are going to let him be in the pasture you promised him. He says you told him he was going to get to move to a big pasture." My mouth dropped open. At the time, Steve and I had purchased eight acres in Arizona where we planned on building a winter home. Smokey was to travel with us and spend the winters on the acreage. I had sent pictures to Smokey and told him he would have more pasture space. I realized, "Shit, she's actually talking with him" and then instantly knew, "He heard me. I communicated with him too."

She passed out brochures for her workshops on animal communication. I took one home, put it on my desk and forgot about it. It got buried under the bills and other mail. A few weeks later, the brochure mysteriously made its way to the top of the pile. I picked it up and realized the workshop was that weekend. I called and signed up for the class.

The workshop was held at the rural home of the animal communicator. She had horses, cats, and dogs, all available for us to communicate with. After talking about energy and explaining to us how communication works, she guided us with a meditation to allow us to connect with an animal. With soft music playing, she said, "Allow your energy to fill the room expanding further out through the roof of the house..." At the first suggestion to expand my energy, I was like a rocket shot out of a cannon. I had been waiting my entire adult life for this invitation. My energy catapulted out of my body and was immediately in the pasture with a horse. I was free and moving without having to lug my body.

Now connected with this horse as if we were one, I could feel his body. I could feel the scratchy discomfort in his throat, a pain in my right foot, suspecting it was his right hind hoof. Along my jaw line I felt soreness, as if someone had scraped the inside of my mouth. All these strange sensations; what did they mean? I could feel warmth in my heart as if I had just been given a big hug. This heart connection was powerful. I wanted to cry.

In a dreamlike state I heard a voice "And now, come back to the room, fully present and here in your body, feeling your feet on the floor." Hearing but resisting, not sure I wanted to leave this beautiful creature and the connection we had, I opened my eyes to a room of people. As our teacher prompted us to share our experience, questions rattled through my mind. "What was that? What just happened? Did I make that up?" I need to know. I'll have to say something or I will never know.

When my turn came, I cautiously described the sensation of slipping out of the room, out of the house and to the pasture. Taking a deep breath I began to explain the sensations I felt, the scratchy throat, the sore foot and the tender jaw. Holding my breath, I noticed the look on my teacher's face. Her eyes widened just a bit as if in surprise, and then a warm knowing smile came across her lips. She began "Yes, the horse you connected with has heaves (a horse condition similar to asthma that creates chronic coughing), and so he often has a scratchy throat. He also had his teeth floated two days ago (horsey dentistry) which explains the jaw line soreness. And yes, he has a stone bruise on his right hind hoof." Holy crap, I thought. What a good guess on my part. I didn't know how to comprehend what I was experiencing. The rest of the day brought more surprises.

I connected with a cat and could clearly feel his nausea. We went around the room each sharing our experience. I began to describe the feelings I noticed while connecting with this cat, and when the words came out of my mouth about the nausea, the cat jumped off the couch and threw up. I was stunned.

Still in disbelief, I decided to put this to a test with another cat. I got quiet and carefully sent him my message. "If I'm really communicating with you, I want proof. I want you to come and sit right in front of me. Then I will know you really heard me and this isn't just a bunch of crap." When our meditation time came to an end, I opened my eyes and saw no cat in front of me. Ha, just as I suspected. I wasn't really communicating with these animals. We went around the room as the other students shared their experiences. When it was my turn, I began to explain my "test" to see if I was actually communicating. I told of how I asked this cat to come to me for proof. As I began talking, the cat came walking in from another room and before I could finish, he sat down directly in front of me looking straight into my eyes. "He couldn't come before because he was busy," the instructor shared. Okay, maybe there was something to this communication thing.

Even though I was just beginning to understand about things like synchronicity and how our soul can send us messages, it was clear to me that I was being asked to pay attention here. This was not a fluke.

As I drove home from the workshop that evening, tears were streaming down my face, burning my cheeks as I heard a small voice inside me say, "Thank God you're finally listening."

A month later I took the Advanced Animal Communication class. Again, I was clearly communicating with the animals. You might think I was thrilled to be able to do this; yet, this time I was very scared. I felt into this fear, not sure where it was coming from when old memories came crashing in. During the abuse involving the pedophile ring, I had been told the abusers had supernatural powers. They convinced my young self they could find me anywhere and would know what I was thinking. They implied they were telepathic. Understanding I clearly was communicating with the animals became twisted in my mind to wondering if I was like them. Would I use my new-found gift for evil purposes? Could they control me? I shared my concerns with my teacher and she assured me this couldn't happen and referred me to a woman who helped me understand the mind control they used on me.

At the end of the class, the teacher took me aside to tell me she gave private lessons. I attended one private lesson with her. Afterwards she shared with me that her business was very busy and she needed help. She asked if she could refer clients to me now. I was sure she was crazy or at least I was. I began practicing with friends' animals as I wasn't as sure of my abilities as she was. After about six months practice and more validation, I let her know I was ready for her to refer clients. This began my professional animal communication career. I worked part-time for the first three years and then left my job at the university to work full time with the animals in 2004.

12

The Teacher in Black

IT WAS EARLY SUMMER 2001 when I met her. We had gone north with a couple of friends to a horsey bed and breakfast of sorts. We had a guest house to ourselves and trails nearby to ride our horses. Smokey was there with me along with his BFF (best friend forever) Nails, a chestnut Arab gelding we trail rode with often.

The guest house was located at an operating ranch with several horses and cattle. On our first day there we noticed the "babies." Two mares had foals by their sides. We all went to meet them. I didn't know this meeting would change my life.

She was beautiful and full of a presence much too grand for a mere three months old. I felt an instant connection to her but didn't understand why. Over the next two days I went back to the barn to see her several times. Finally, on the last day she clearly communicated to me, you know we are supposed to be together. "You need to find her and talk to her about buying me." What? Although I had been consciously communicating with animals for about a year, this awareness of her feelings took me by surprise.

My rational mind played it out like this. I had no desire for a second horse…sure I knew I would need another horse in a few years to keep Smokey company, but I never considered getting a baby and certainly not a mare. I didn't even know if she was for sale. She was a black Appaloosa and Tennessee Walking Horse (TWH) cross, although without any white markings, so she couldn't be registered. Her sire was a very tall spotted black and white TWH. At five feet two, I didn't need a tall horse. It was a crapshoot as to whether she would be gaited like a TWH. Nothing about this made logical sense. And yet, I couldn't stop thinking about her. I felt her in my heart, not my head.

When I approached the woman who owned the ranch to see if the filly was for sale, she told me her name was Mariah, and that she had been born on a full moon, on a very windy night. She came sooner than they expected, so she was born outside with no humans around. She might consider selling her. She would need to figure out what she had invested to determine her price. We exchanged contact information.

The next week the phone call came. The owner had considered her investment and determined a price. It was not reasonable. This little filly was "grade" and not yet a weanling but she was asking close to what I paid for Smokey, a trained registered Tennessee Walking Horse with excellent bloodlines. I told her I would think about it and get back to her. The money wasn't the issue. Even though it wasn't market value, it was affordable for me.

For the next week, my logical mind was in a battle with my heart. Back and forth I went. I don't remember struggling so much over a decision. Finally, a good friend of mine who had listened to me go back and forth with this for a week said to me, "BUY HER." Why, I asked? "Because every time you talk about her your entire being lights up. To me that means you need to do this…set your logic aside and listen to your heart." I knew she was right. And just so I didn't back out, she followed me to my office while I made the call to tell the owner I would accept her price.

Apparently, I called the owner's bluff. She purposely set the price high because she wasn't sure she wanted to part with her. She too felt her presence and knew there was something special about this filly. But she agreed to the sale, and in another two months, Mariah was delivered to me.

Now you might expect me to tell you she is the most wonderful horse I've ever known and we ride off onto the trails until sunset. Not the case. She has been the most challenging horse I have ever known, and, at the same time, one of the greatest blessings in my life.

When she arrived at the stables where I was boarding Smokey, she first needed to be quarantined in a stall for two weeks. She kicked a friend who was feeding her the first day she arrived. Mariah's original owner explained "she came out of her mother kicking," meaning she had been kicking since she first saw a human. She kicked out at many people, but never, ever me. Difficult as she was, we had a strong heart connection and I knew she trusted me.

During the day I would take her out to give her some fresh air in the stallion pen. I remember sitting there one day waiting for a friend to come join me. When my friend arrived, she told me we needed to listen to the news on the radio. Something had happened in New York. A plane had crashed into a building. That was September 11th, 2001. My friend and I listened to the radio and both decided we needed to get back to our homes and families.

After her quarantine, Mariah was moved to the pasture with a group of other weanlings. She continued to be a challenge and was quickly gaining a bad reputation, so I moved her to a stable near Janesville owned by a competent natural horse trainer. I knew she would be handled daily and would live outside in a mixed herd. There she could be a horse and I was able to work with her with guidance from the trainer.

An equine body worker who found her challenging told me the name Mariah meant devil and I should change her name. I've never found any association with Mariah and devil. The Hebrew derivative, Moriah means "teacher," the Native American word Moriah, means "the wind." Intuitively I knew her name was perfect as were her clear boundaries and unwillingness to submit to being told what to do rather than being asked.

Her first experience with the farrier was a scene from the farrier's course of "how to be patient with a young horse." She started kicking towards him before he even came close. Shortly after, I began learning how to do a natural trim myself. With guidance from my teacher, I trimmed her hooves. It wasn't easy to trim a moving target but she never kicked at me and eventually she stood still.

As difficult as she was, I wasn't afraid of her. One day, while working with her in the round pen, she reared strait up directly in front of me. She could have come down and killed me I suppose, but I knew she wouldn't. I understood because of our connection she thought she and I should play the rearing game like Smokey and Nails did. I had to laugh. And then of course I sent her out away from me to let her know we weren't playing a game.

Shortly after she came into my life, I was led to the book, *The Tao of Equus*, by Linda Kohanov. Linda tells the story of a black Arabian mare whom she met as a filly, with hopes of riding her in upper level dressage and endurance. As circumstances unfolded, an injury to her mare dashed her dreams. Her mare had a much more important role to play in her life. Through a series of events, dreams, and what we call the supernatural, this mare led Linda to her life's work of Equine Facilitated Learning through her internationally known business EponaQuest Worldwide. Horses mirror the emotions of the people around them. Because of this, they are now used in a variety of therapeutic ways to help humans.

Mariah has taught me more about horsemanship than the many clinics, books, and videos I studied. More significantly, she has taught me the importance of having clear boundaries and how to be in my power while remaining quiet. I knew when she came into my life that she was here to help me understand power and to show me a healthy balance of the feminine and masculine. But first, she needed me to see my buried rage.

This was the most valuable lesson of all. There was a rage deep inside of me fostered by years of unfair treatment and abuse where I was unable to fight back. As a young child, I was terrified but could not express the unfairness of it all. The rage inside me was building like hot lava in a volcano and I was trying everything possible to keep it hidden from myself. After all, it's not okay to be angry. Good girls don't get mad. Men who get angry are assertive; women are bitches.

When Mariah was 15, I moved her and Smokey from the farm and herd they had known for 12 years to a boarding stable. The decision was forced on me. It was difficult for all of us. In this less stable environment, Mariah became more and more difficult to handle. She did not feel secure and I was not helping her to feel secure. She is a very strong horse and her fearful actions caused me injuries on a few occasions and I worried for the safety of others. I didn't know what to do with her. I considered selling her but who would purchase such a willful and uncooperative horse? And the thought of selling her dropped me to my knees in sorrow. I tried a couple of trainers without much success. Understanding that our animals are mirrors to our own emotions, I kept wondering what more I needed to learn from her. One day, she was being dangerously uncooperative and I lost it. I yelled and hit her with the lead rope. I was so angry at her and then the "aha" moment happened. I saw how my fear was connected to my rage. When she did anything that scared me I wanted to strike back. I wanted to attack her like I was never able to do to my abusers. I was in a state of rage. I cried when I realized the angry woman I had become.

This was a turning point for me. I was now able to acknowledge my buried rage. I communicated with her that I finally understood what she had been trying to teach me. I was able to stop the fear/rage cycle when I was with her and began to use my energy with her in a new way. Instead of trying to force my energy on her, or make my energy bigger, I softened my energy field to coexist (not comingle) with hers. I did not need to be the "herd leader" or the "boss" to gain her cooperation. I needed to be trustworthy and safe.

She is still a strong spirit who refuses to be conquered, unjustly controlled, or a slave to another's desires. She hates being ridden, so I no longer expect it from her. She will cooperate, but only as a partnership where each individual is respected. Though she is strong and willful, she is also loving when I am in a peaceful state. She came to show me it's possible to stand up for myself and get cooperation from another without using force or manipulation. She taught me how to use my energy and intention to communicate clearly. She taught me to take back my power.

We may expect someone who has been abused to be afraid of others who abuse power. The unexpected piece is that we are often also afraid of our own power, because we fear we will become like those who abused us, and if we don't acknowledge our rage, we can become like them. We give up our power and remain victim to another's will until we learn to recognize our buried rage and use our power in constructive and cooperative ways.

As a Fractured Phoenix, it is likely you have experienced powerlessness. As a young child, surrendering may have been your only option. This was true for me. Now, we can take back our power and it may surprise you just what this involves. Following is a list of ways to take back your power.

- Live in the present moment. All your power is here, right now in this moment. There is nothing for you in the past or the undetermined future.
- Be embodied and energetically contained. Bringing all your energy back to you and grounding will engage your personal power (details are provided in chapter 28).
- Acknowledge your rage; know that you are entitled to it and find a way to release it safely.
- Do not allow external circumstances to control your emotions, your feelings, or your decisions and actions.
- Make your own decisions without allowing others to make decisions for you, either directly or indirectly.
- Know yourself and what you truly desire and need (this helps greatly with decision making).
- Trust yourself, your abilities, your goodness and your value.
- Give up people pleasing. This can be challenging as pleasing was essential to our early survival. This is no longer true. Others can be unhappy

with your decisions ... you will not die from their disapproval. Not everyone needs to like you.

- Offer your unique gifts to the world. Each of us came here with unique gifts to share with the world. You can discover yours by going within to your stillness.

13

From Communicating to Healing

DURING THE FIRST ANIMAL COMMUNICATION class I attended, I was also introduced to essential oils from one of the other students. Though I was usually sensitive to fragrances and couldn't tolerate the smell of perfumes, the essential oils had an opposite effect on me. I couldn't get enough. I learned some basics about essential oils and used them on my dog, Tiger. I was surprised by how an oil blend changed Tiger's fear of thunderstorms. At the time, I didn't know the importance of diluting the oils and offering them to an animal, not just applying them without the animal's permission. This was not taught by the essential oil company distributor who had been providing me guidance. Not knowing better, I continued to put the oil blend on his paws after he had improved without asking. After doing this several times he began refusing to let me get close with the oils. I finally understood him. He was telling me he no longer wanted or needed the oils.

My desire to learn more about using essential oils with animals led me to Nayana Morag, who would become my mentor and friend. Through her Certification program for Animal Essential Oil Therapy (now referred to as Animal PsychAromatica through The Essential School of Balance), I learned how our animals know innately what they need. After two years of study, I became one of the first Certified Animal Aromatherapists in the US. The method I learned in choosing essential oils to support an animal physically, energetically, and emotionally involved concepts of Traditional Chinese Medicine. Once certified, I began helping animals with essential oils as well as animal communication.

This direction with my work was confirmed during a meditation at Unity one Sunday afternoon. We were being guided through a meditation and encouraged to ask a question. Without any forethought, the question came to me, "How can I serve?" The answer came quickly in a voice not my own, "Heal the animals." It was so clear, so out of the blue I knew it was my Soul no longer whispering, but shouting to me.

About the same time, I found myself being drawn to placing my hands on my horses and allowing energy to flow. This strong desire was difficult to resist. I wasn't trained in any specific modality, but was working from intuition. When I was with the horses, I would ground myself by bringing my attention inward and imagine roots growing out of my feet into the earth. With my attention focused on my heart center, I began to feel energy flow out of my hands. I stayed present in my body sensing where my hands were needed, without controlling or directing the energy. I followed this subtle direction until the energy stopped flowing through my hands. Sometimes the horses would release emotion or show me pictures of a previous trauma. The sessions often resulted in significant improvement of the horse's physical and behavioral issues.

I was also guided towards healing after a remarkable situation with my dog King. King was only nine weeks old when the seizures started. This tiny toy poodle of two and a half pounds had already stolen my heart. I recognized the flailing legs and odd body contortions as a seizure, having lived through it before with my dog Boo Boo. The first episode came as my then partner and I drove back from a Sunday trip to Madison. We pulled off the interstate at the next exit, the small town of Bancroft. I ran into the BP gas station to ask about the nearest emergency vet. They recommended Stevens Point, which is where we were already headed. I began calling all the vets in the area and found a vet who would meet us at the Amherst Vet Clinic. We arrived and I shared what happened.

After examining him, the vet felt he hadn't had a seizure but he did have an ear infection. She gave us medicine for the ear and sent us on our way. In a way, I felt relieved, but the scene lingered in my mind and part of me knew it had been a seizure. In the wee hours of the morning, King had two more seizures. Upon wakening, I took him to my regular vet and called a friend (who was also a vet) to get her advice. She recommended getting him to the nearest neurologist.

When I got to my vet, he made some calls to UW Madison, but the neurologist would not be in for several days. Our next best option was the Fox Valley Referral Center in Appleton. We drove the 45 miles to Appleton. My heart raced. My mind followed with "how could a dog so young have seizures? Did he get into something toxic? What was to become of this tiny, precious life?"

The triage nurse quickly assessed the situation and he was admitted and placed on seizure watch. He had four more seizures in the next 36 hours. Seven seizures so far in 48 hours. His tiny, short life was terribly uncertain. To assess what might be causing the seizures, they began a multitude of tests including a cerebral spinal tap. My partner and I left him in their capable hands feeling helpless to do anything else.

The next day we drove to visit him and get the test results. As we exited the last ramp, a deep unexpected peace came over me. There was a shift in my being

I didn't quite understand, yet I was grateful for the break from worrying.

Arriving at the hospital, we were greeted by the vet assistant. "When the Dr. took the spinal tap there was a complication. Because he's so tiny, she inadvertently poked his brain stem with the needle. As a result, there was blood in the sample so we are unable to use the sample. He's also having some neurological issues that may be the result of the spinal tap or could be the progression of the disease." My heart sank. My gut knew it wasn't the progression of any disease, but the result of the spinal tap.

She took us into a small private room, brought King in and left us alone. We set him on the floor and he walked lilting to the left as if his left hind leg had been pinned to the ground. This was not the puppy we brought in. My partner and I sat down facing each other. Though I had never taken a Reiki or other energy healing class, I knew what needed to be done. I placed King on my lap, gently laying my hands on him. Pulsating energy began to flow through my heart center and out my hands to King. The vibration intensified, and my being was overtaken with sounds and chants I'd never uttered before. Deep, visceral indigenous sounds gushed out from the depths of my diaphragm. All self-consciousness was gone. After about 10 minutes, the vibration began to slow, the chanting ceased. With confidence, I looked at my partner and knew we were done.

Shortly after, the veterinarian came into the room. He placed King on the table and conducted a few neurological tests. "Well," he said, "his neurological issues are improving. He's doing much better already. I think it might be best for him if we sent him home with you. He will be less stressed."

We took King home, and two days later I drove to Madison to see the Neurologist at the UW Veterinary College. An MRI revealed a swollen brain stem from the spinal tap. No other pathologies were found in his brain. All other tests were negative. The only potential cause never ruled out was a reaction to the vaccinations King had received twelve days prior to the first seizure. After the healing session, King never had another seizure. The neurological symptoms were completely gone after 4 days. King was never vaccinated again.

14

Our Initiation

WHEN I LEARNED ABOUT SHAMANS of Indigenous tribes and the initiations they endured to fully embrace their healing abilities, it occurred to me their initiation experiences parallel that of a survivor of childhood trauma. It is said a true Shaman must face the Spirit of Death, a dark Spirit that comes to him or her and must be faced with love rather than fear. Overcoming the Spirit of Death is an essential component of their initiation. Only then can they walk in the other worlds to assist the healing of others.

For a survivor, at least as a young child like myself, there were several times during my early childhood when I felt as if I was facing death. However, I wouldn't meet the Spirit of Death until I was in my thirties and processing the memories I had buried so long ago.

I awoke to a dark, ominous presence. I could feel this black energy lift me and slam me into the ceiling of the bedroom. I was terrified. This felt real. I knew I needed to fight this or I wouldn't survive. I repeated the Lord's Prayer over and over. "Our Father, who art in heaven, hallowed be thy Name, thy kingdom come, thy will be done, on earth as it is in heaven. Give us this day our daily bread. And forgive us our trespasses, as we forgive those who trespass against us. And lead us not into temptation, but deliver us from evil. For thine is the kingdom, and the power, and the glory, for ever and ever. Amen."

Reciting the prayer was instinctual. This...whatever this was...felt satanic and evil. Every inch of me knew I had to fight the evil; I had to resist this satanic being. All I could think of was to recite the prayer. And the prayer worked. Eventually, I fell back onto the bed. I had won ... this time but this black presence would return again. Again, I would recite the prayer. This happened on and off over a few years and eventually stopped. I assumed this recurring nightmare was my psyche working through the pain of the abuse memories, as if my subconscious was somehow making sense of the blackness of the buried memories. I was convinced only God could save me. Surely I must be dreaming this, but was I?

At the time, it didn't occur to me that this was anything but a nightmare…a subconscious mind trying to make sense of the senseless…until I read about the initiation process of Shamans from indigenous cultures. Even then, it didn't seem that it could be anything more than a nightmare because I don't believe in Satan. I don't believe in evil spirits. I do believe humans have done evil deeds. But I don't believe we *are* evil. We are spirits and the evil in our world is a manifestation of our own fears and wounds. We create evil and "evil spirits" from our thoughts, and with our thoughts we can create the opposite of evil. But if we are so engaged with the illusion of evil, it can become very difficult to dissolve that illusion.

What if this was the Black Spirit that came to initiate me into Shamanism? Was this the opening to my healing abilities? Perhaps all the torture, hurts, and betrayals were my initiation.

For those of us who have burned in the fires of abuse, there seems to be the ability to channel healing energy more successfully than others. I have no scientific evidence to back this up, but my experience working with healers has shown a significant majority have experienced early childhood trauma. It's my theory that by becoming an empath early in life (out of necessity), the ability to hold an open channel to funnel healing energy from Source is enhanced. I liken it to blowing up a balloon. The first time you blow into a new balloon, the rubber is tight and it takes more effort. The more you blow up that same balloon, the more the rubber loosens and allows air to flow more easily and quickly. Those of us who have been sending our energy out to read others seem to be "loosening the balloon" and increasing our capacity to allow energy to flow through us. If you have felt the pull to be a healer, understand you stand with many other Fractured Phoenixes. Your early life experiences were your initiation. The capacity of your heart when open knows no bounds.

Learning From Loss

MY SWEET DOG TIGER, a Lhasa/Maltese, passed into Spirit June 22, 2004 and provided me lessons in love, loss and reincarnation.

Tiger was the guardian of the house. Though small in stature, he was very large in courage. He had many fears: loud noises, vacuum cleaners, things out of place, yet he never let those fears stop him. Instead, he would ferociously protect me and our home. One of the funniest quirks he had was watching television. He would sit with me and watch the television intently. Tiger was quickly in front of the TV screen whenever a dog showed up on the TV, however slight or small, even just a bark in the background. With his front paws on the TV and back legs planted firmly, he barked and howled at those dogs on the other side of the "window." At first I asked him not to bark, but then I realized how important his job was to him, and so his barking became music to my ears.

Tiger was eleven years old when he cracked a tooth, requiring surgery. I connected with Tiger about the upcoming surgery. I let him know what to expect and that afterwards the pain would go away. During his surgery, I connected with him again to reassure him the pain from the tooth would be gone. When I connected with him, he was out of his body and I knew he wanted to leave, to go to the light. Frightened of losing my closest four-legged companion, I said, "No, please, don't go to the light. I need you here; you are my best little man." He felt my desperation and went back into his body. I disconnected from his energy, trusting he decided to stay.

Shortly thereafter, the vet called to tell me everything had gone fine, Tiger was awake and I could pick him up. I didn't think anymore about him leaving his body, I was just grateful he decided to stay. When I picked him up at the vet, I thought he looked fine, but when we arrived home I knew something was very wrong. Without going into all the details, Tiger began having complications.

I took him back to the vet that evening and then again the next morning. The vet thought he was having an allergic reaction to something given to him during the surgery and gave him some medicine to counteract the reaction. They expected him to be better soon, but he wasn't getting better.

We went home and I watched Tiger get worse. For the rest of the day, I tried to help him be comfortable as I watched him leave his body and come back. I tried to visualize him trotting down the driveway on our walks to the mailbox or running around stealing horse "apples." Deep inside me, I knew he was leaving me and there was nothing I could do to bring him back. Every once in awhile he would come back and do something very "Tiger" as best he could. I considered taking him to a specialist but I knew in my heart that western medicine could do no more for him. I trusted the prayers would work and couldn't think about other possibilities. I offered him some helichrysum essential oil to help him with the pain and he became much more peaceful.

It was about 10:30 at night when our toy poodle Maddie began frantically barking, waking us up. Tiger was lying at my feet gasping his last breath. I picked up his limp body and felt his heart beating but he was gone. I tried to revive him with CPR even though I knew he wasn't in his body. I pleaded for him to come back, but it was not to be. Within moments his heart stopped beating as he passed away in my arms. Peacefulness came over me and I realized his spirit was still with me even though it had left his body.

I held Tiger in my arms for two hours until we decided it was time to bury his body. My partner dug a hole by a grove of trees near our deck. The night was beautiful and clear, lit up by the moon and stars. We put his little red jacket on him embroidered with "Run Hard Bark Loud," which was the essence of his existence. Gently we placed his body in the grave along with special tokens to honor him ... Frankincense, sage, a crystal, a feather, special toys, and treats. An owl spoke as if in prayer. My tears became rivers as my cries echoed off the surrounding land. Just then, a pack of coyotes joined in singing a lengthy hymn for Tiger. It was a sacred and beautiful crossing over the Rainbow Bridge where all our beloved animals go when they leave Earth.

The next day a small voice inside made me realize the date was important. Looking in Tiger's file, I found the paperwork from when I first got him, June 21, 1993. On the exact day and month he came into my life, he planned on leaving, but he stayed an extra day at my request. He spared me from getting a call from the vet saying he died in surgery. I was given one more day to be with him and hold him as he crossed over completely. He planned to go on exactly the same day and month he came into my life so I would know *this was our agreement.*

Our Souls made an agreement before we came to this lifetime. It was his time to go; his lessons and work here were done. I was guided to check the dates so I could be reassured there were no coincidences. There was nothing I could have or should have done differently.

Two weeks after his passing I had the opportunity to have a photograph taken of my aura (energy field). It was a new and fascinating experience, especially when the woman explaining the colors and their significance (who didn't know me at all) told me there was another energy field enmeshed in mine, a very small one. With tears welling in my eyes I told her "Yes, that's my dog Tiger who recently crossed into Spirit." And in the photo, I could see a small golden color orb over my aura.

Even though I could feel his spirit, I still missed him physically. He communicated with me and helped me with my work, assuring me he could be with me and in the other realms as well.

In his passing, Tiger gave me a precious gift. He was a reminder for my belief there are no accidents or coincidences. Those who come into our lives, whether they are two- or four-legged, are here for a reason. They are part of a divine plan we cannot possibly understand nor do we need to. I believe he intended for me to share this message. Our animals are here for a reason and for a specific time. They are here to help us learn to love ourselves and to love others. When their work here on Earth is done, they will leave us. Be grateful for the time you have with them. Treat them with kindness and listen with your heart open. When you cross over into Spirit, they will be waiting for you.

Seven months later, I was conducting an introductory animal communication class during which I guide the students through a meditation and communication experience. During the pause created for them to connect with one of their animals, I asked my own animals if anyone needed anything. Tiger's spirit came in and greeted me with a very matter-of-fact "I'm coming back." "What? You're coming back?" "Yes", he said, "very soon." I was almost in shock. I told him how happy and excited I was, and asked him to please look as much as possible like he did as Tiger. He shared he was coming back to help me with my work, to help heal the animals. This time though, he wouldn't need the trials and lessons of his former life and so he was coming back without the painful early experiences of a puppy mill. This time, a happy, healthy "puppyhood" would support his work and lessons.

As my students shared their experiences, I too shared with tears and excitement. Tiger is coming back. Where, when, and how he will come back didn't seem to matter. I knew Tiger would be back with me soon. A heavy weight was lifted off my heart.

In a lifetime we can connect with and love many animals, but certain Souls (for whatever reason) connect more than others. Tiger was like a Soul mate to me. I'm not sure what it is that distinguishes one heart connection from another, but this was much deeper, a knowingness, a connection, an understanding. He looked right through me; he understood my deepest feelings, my fears, and my joys. He was the one who urged me back to my childhood ability to communicate with the animals. It wasn't until years later I recognized how subtle he had been…staring, piercing me with his thoughts and emotions, urging me to listen. I remember sitting in my office, working on my computer, staring into the monitor and feeling as if he were screaming at me. I would turn around and find him staring at me with an intensity that caused his body to tremble. "Get away from that stupid machine and come play with me," he seemed to say. I chuckle at how many times he tried to get through to me before I finally "got it."

Two months later as I was checking my email, I saw the subject "puppies" from a woman who has brought me two dogs. She was not a professional breeder, but someone who had an exceptionally loving, intelligent and physically healthy female toy poodle and had decided to have two litters of puppies. In the email, the woman explained she had already scheduled the spaying of her toy poodle, Ebony, when she received a call from a woman who desperately wanted a female puppy of her lineage. The breeder explained the male had been neutered. "No problem" was the response;

she had a sire in mind, a Maltese. (Remember, Tiger was a Lhasa/Maltese cross). And so an agreement was reached. Ebony was bred one last time to a Maltese.

As I read the email and came to the word "Maltese," it hit me. "Oh my God, it's Tiger; he's coming back in this litter as a Malti-poo." My heart is beating fast, tears well up in my eyes, joy explodes through my body. I'm so excited I can hardly think straight. I panic. I need confirmation. This is so important. I call my friend and mentor. She telepathically checks in with the litter of puppies and confirms what I already know, Tiger is back. (Typically animal communicators do get help from each other when it involves one's own animal in a highly emotional situation). My inner guides kick in. "Go back to the email, check the date." And so I re-read the email. One female puppy was born before midnight, the others after, on February 22nd. Exactly eight months to the day Tiger left, he came back. Once again, he wanted me to be sure if I had any doubts, the date clue would guide me.

From my discussion with my friend, we were certain he was a boy, light colored, and big. There were three boys, one black, one little white one, and one chubby white and tan one. I sent an email back to the breeder to let her know I wanted the chubby tan and white boy. I telepathically connected in with Tiger, now in a little baby body but he was busy! He said "Mmmmm, more milk," and began drinking from his mother. He wasn't interested in talking at the moment! Later, I had another communication with him about what he wanted his name to be. He told me "Doc," Doctor Doolittle. My partner was "listening" at the same time and heard "Doodle". So "Doc," aka Doctor Doolittle, it was.

I was able to visit him for the first time in person when he was about three weeks of age. I was very excited as I walked into the home and could feel Tiger's energy. By this time, I had become used to feeling his energy with me, but his energy felt a bit different now. I could also feel and hear his new youthfulness come through. It's as though you are connecting to two animals when an animal Soul comes through a new body. There is the familiar and wise Soul you know so well and then there's the personality/ego of the new puppy which will pop in occasionally as well. It is all part of the process of reincarnating back into a body with the Soul or "higher self" having a more prominent role in the beginning. This "higher self" then begins to step back a bit as the new personality comes through to experience puppyhood.

When the puppies were about eight weeks old, it was time to pick up Doc. I cried tears of joy as I made the drive to bring Doc/Tiger back home.

Tiger was excited to be back with me and this family. He came back more quickly than is typical; explaining his time "between lives" was quite easy. This lifetime he wanted to experience coming into a healthy body, undamaged physically, and emotionally to a loving family. He experienced what it is like to be a puppy with loving siblings, to not be left alone or neglected but completely loved, nurtured, and protected. This time his body is strong and healthy, not riddled with complications from vaccinosis. He experienced all the joys of puppyhood as a healthy, well socialized, little guy.

The name he chose was no accident. I soon discovered he had a gift for helping me and the animals by selecting essential oils. It began when he picked an oil for himself. Sniffing over the large tray of closed bottles, he stopped, picked up one particular oil with his mouth, and then set it down. It was exactly what he needed. I was prompted to ask him what another dog I was working with needed. Without hesitation, he went back to the tray, sniffed only a brief second and picked up a bottle with his mouth. I looked at the oil he chose; it was one of the top three picks for this situation.

As I review all that transpired since Tiger first came into my life in 1993, clearly he was here to help me with my work. He taught me so much. With his special needs as a puppy, he took me on a path to learn about holistic care for animals: the problems of over-vaccination, commercial diets, and food allergies. He also reminded me of the miracles western medicine can offer during his ordeal with a herniated disk in his neck and the surgery that saved him. And it was his persistence in communicating with me that returned me to my Soul's path of talking with the animals to help them heal. Through his passing, he allowed me to experience what it feels like to be with a Soul as it transitions to the other side, and to feel that Soul's energy with me even when the physical body was no longer there. I experienced being able to call upon the Soul for comfort as I grieved the loss of his physical presence, and I witnessed the graceful dance of the Soul and the new personality as he came back to me in his new body. What an amazing teacher he has been.

At one point I began to wonder if I was meant to expand the healing work or focus only on the Animal Communication and essential oil work. I decided to pray for guidance. One night with intention and knowledge that my question would be answered, I asked, "What am I to do with healing for animals? Please provide some direction if I am meant to do energy healing." The next day, I opened up my emails and found an invitation for a course on Equine Craniosacral Therapy. I looked at the program and knew this was the answer. Craniosacral Therapy uses an intuitive light touch and energy to recalibrate the rhythm of the cerebral spinal fluid. Conveniently, the course was being sponsored by someone I knew not far away. Even though I didn't have the funds at the time, I trusted this was meant to be and signed up for the course. When it was time to pay for the class, the funds showed up.

I took two courses from this instructor, and later, a human course in Craniosacral Therapy as well. The first time I drove to work on a client's horse, I felt a deep peace and joy, knowing I was doing what I was called to do. The craniosacral work provided a path for me to share the intuitive healing energy flowing through me. The changes in the horses and dogs I worked on were often remarkable.

Carl Jung coined the term "synchronicity" to express the concept of coincidence that scientific rationality could not make clear. Synchronicity is the phenomenon of the alignment of universal forces with one's own life experiences; a cluster of meaningful patterns that normal cause and effect has not caused. Synchronicity is beyond cause as we know it: a bridge between the known and the unknown, between the conscious and the unconscious. Jung suggests (and I believe) these "coincidences" have a deeper meaning and are messages from the universe, our Soul or God/ Source. We are often given signs and guidance. When we want guidance and direction, we need to ask. And then when we act on the guidance, we can trust more guidance will show up.

16

Cosmic Acupuncture

As I WONDERED ABOUT where my strong desire to do energy healing with animals was coming from, I realized the urge began a few years before, after my healing sessions with Rubens Faria, a psychic healer from Brazil. Finding this healer was like many other experiences in my life, a synchronistic intervention by my Soul.

The healing happened during the summer as I was planning a trip to Colorado to attend the Horse Gathering, a weeklong conference on natural horse training and care put together by Mark Rashid, author and clinician.

Early in the week, I woke in the middle of the night with excruciating pain radiating down my leg. The pain was so intense I sobbed. The next morning, still in pain, I received a call from a good friend who was going to be in my area with another mutual friend. Although my pain was intense, these friends always provided me with the laughter I needed. I invited them over. As we sat out on the back patio laughing and reminiscing I told them about my pain. My friend Alex mentioned there was a man at the Miracles Healing Center performing healing. In fact, he had seen the man the day before and had received a "treatment" for an old knee injury from years of playing basketball. His description of the man digging into his knee with no more than a broken can opener gave me chills. Yet he swore he felt no pain and his knee was completely without pain for the first time in years. He talked of others having cataracts removed by having their eyeballs scraped with a scalpel...all without any anesthesia or sedation. All without pain. These accounts of bloodless, painless surgeries seemed hard to believe and yet, I knew there was a reason he was here on this day, when I was in this horrible pain telling me about these healings. He said he could get me in and made a couple of calls. I was scheduled to see the healer the next day.

The healing center was about an hour north of my home. I had no expectations, but admittedly was hesitant. The pain shooting down my leg was enough to keep me driving in spite of the unknown. I was aware this place was an academy for those studying A Course in Miracles, and rumors were that the center was a cult of some sort. This didn't concern me. I knew my friend well and had studied a Course in Miracles. Marianne Williamson's first book, *A Return to Love*, was based on a Course in Miracles. The book and my further studies of the Course was part of my healing process and I embraced its teachings.

When I arrived, there were about 50 people in a round room that served as a type of chapel. I was told I would need to wait awhile. I could see a procession of people go into and out of some rooms further down a hallway. There were small meditation rooms off the big round chapel. Shortly after my arrival, my friend greeted me and we joined the group in the chapel. Group prayer was taking place but not the kind of prayer I had grown up with in the Lutheran church. This wasn't about taking away our sins. This was about opening our hearts to love one another. The energy of love was enormous. We sang, we laughed, and we blissed out on the high vibration created from this group of loving Souls.

The feeling of love and peace from this energy reminded me of a time when I was driving down the road on a beautiful spring day in 2000. In a moment, a flash really, I could feel my connection to all life. There was no separation between the trees, plants, animals, clouds, and me. It was intense bliss. The colors were more vibrant and beautiful than I had ever seen before. It was a magical moment of love and bliss...but only a moment. This type of experience is referred to in Eastern philosophy traditions as "Ecstasy of Unity." It's also known as "religious ecstasy." In 1971, after walking on the moon, Apollo 14 Astronaut Edgar Mitchell was returning to Earth when he experienced this ecstasy of unity. He wrote: *"There seems to be more to the universe than random, chaotic, purposeless movement of a collection of molecular particles. On the return trip home, gazing through 240,000 miles of space towards the stars and the planet from which I had come, I suddenly experienced the universe as intelligent, loving, and harmonious. I experienced an ecstasy of unity. I not only saw the connectedness, I felt it and experienced it sentiently. The restraints and boundaries of flesh and bone fell away."*

In this chapel of the Miracles Healing Center, I experienced a feeling almost as blissful, but which lasted much longer. After what seemed like thirty minutes, my name was called. I checked my watch. Three hours had passed.

A woman came out and greeted me. She explained she would be with me through the entire process; she had been assigned to guide and care for me. First, I was taken to a room where they asked me questions about my concerns. I explained about the pain shooting down my leg. They encouraged me to share anything else that might need healing. With a bit of skepticism and at the same time hope, I decided to lay out every ailment and issue I had ever endured. I shared that I was hypothyroid and had suffered for years from depression. I had been diagnosed with fibromyalgia and chronic fatigue years earlier. I wasn't currently experiencing any symptoms but just in case those two syndromes were lurking and sleeping somewhere in my system, I decided to get rid of all illness that had ever plagued me. They took notes and then escorted me into the treatment room. The room was about 20' x 25', with a circle of massage tables all occupied by other hopeful patients. Off to the side were mats on the floor where people were resting.

There he was. Rubens Faria. He was about 5'8", maybe in his late 30s, with dark hair and a slight build. I learned when he performed the treatments, he channeled a Dr. Fritz, who lived in Germany decades before. He was not the first to channel this being. According to the story, Rubens had been an engineer, with no particular spiritual calling, when his young daughter became very ill. When he was in the hospital with her and it looked like she would not live, he prayed to God to please save her. He would do anything. Without a conversation of what was to come, the daughter recovered. Weeks later, Rubens unexpectedly fell into a trance, and while in trance, he healed another person. He had no recollection of what happened while in the trance, but this was the beginning of his healing as Dr.

Fritz. He gave up his work as an engineer and dedicated his life to healing.

Others gathered around him, following directions and assisting as he moved from table to table. I was led to a table and asked to lie down. I could see him at the next table where an older, heavy set man was lying. On one side, he had a port of some sort coming out of his abdomen draining a fluid into a vessel. I could hear parts of the conversation. A tumor, located on the opposite side of where the draining was occurring, was being addressed. Something about how even though the tumor was on the right side, it needed to drain on the left side. I could see him clearly and I couldn't imagine where the fluid was coming from, and yet it was draining out of his body into the vial.

Then he came to me.

His assistants spoke to him in Portuguese. He looked at me with deep brown eyes radiating compassion and love. My shirt had two ribbons at the neckline that had come untied. He tied them in a little bow and smiled at me. Then he took out what looked like a large acupuncture needle and jabbed the needle into my upper thigh, right through my jeans. "Ouch," I said. In English he said, "I'm sorry there will be some pain yet." That was the extent of his work on me and he walked to the next table. I lay there for about 15 minutes when he came back and removed the needle. He said something again in Portuguese to one of the assistants. His assistant turned to me and said, "He would like you to come again tomorrow." I said okay, not really knowing how I would fit in another trip, given I was preparing to leave for Colorado in two days. My helper woman was now at my side and helped me over to one of the mats. She told me to rest for a while and she would return to fetch me. After she came back, we made arrangements for me to return the next day. There was no charge for any of this service, but I chose to make a donation to the Miracles Healing Center.

As I drove home I could still feel the pain in my leg. My fears set in.

I'll probably turn on 60 Minutes and find out what a big hoax and fraud this guy is. How could I buy into this? I'm an intelligent, college educated woman. What was I thinking? At the same time, another part of me knew something very remarkable happened. Something shifted, even if the pain was still there.

That night as I lay in bed, still in pain, I remembered a teaching from a Course in Miracles. I prayed "Dear God, please let me see this differently." After about 15 minutes, my pain changed. The pain didn't go away completely, but instead became more of a sensation and less of pain. I slept well for the first time in a long while.

The next morning, I was scheduled to meet with an energy worker I was seeing every other week. I had just enough time for our appointment before my trip back to the Miracle Healing Center. I was glad I could see my wise mentor, because my fears and mistrusts of the healing were creeping back in. I told my healer friend all about my experience the previous day and wondered what she thought. I trusted her judgment more than my own, as was often the case back then.

She shared a story about how years ago she had a large cyst in her abdomen. She tried every holistic method she could find to deal with it. Nothing seemed to help. She learned about a healer, much like Rubens Faria, who was in the US, but she did not have the funds to fly to where he was. Then, a friend gifted her with all she needed to visit this healer. When she arrived, she was excited, believing this would solve her problem. The healer told her the tumor was too large to deal with and she should have surgery to have the growth removed. While the experience wasn't what she originally expected, she shared with me that a profound Spiritual healing did take place for her. This gave me comfort about my decision to return to the Miracle Healing Center later that day.

When I arrived, again, I spent some time in the chapel. My time with the prayer circle was much shorter this time, and soon I was escorted back into the large healing room and placed on a massage table. When Rubens came by he placed the large acupuncture needle in my leg again, smiled, and walked off. I thought, "I'm having another cosmic acupuncture session." After about 20 minutes, he came back to me and removed the needle. He said a few things in Portuguese to his assistants, then looked deeply into my eyes and said "Everything will be okay."

There are no words to express what I felt as he spoke to me. I was looking into his eyes and I truly felt as if I was looking into the eyes of the Divine. I have no other way to explain the immense feeling of peace and unconditional love that swept over me at that moment. I said "Thank you" with tears welling in the corners of my eyes. The memory still brings tears of gratitude.

My attendant helped me off the table and walked with me to a mat on the floor. She told me "He has requested to see you again. You must have very important work to do." But in my mind I was thinking, "I must be really fucked up to need all these sessions." I was told Rubens was traveling to California in two days, but would return again after several days to Wisconsin.

I drove home with an overwhelming feeling of peace. Worries about my newly purchased young filly were gone. I knew no matter what happened, everything in my life would be okay. I was in love with the world around me and with myself. This feeling lived in me for another ten-twelve months. I was at peace with whatever came my way.

17

The Heartache of Following Your Truth

MY EXCITEMENT ABOUT MY EXPERIENCE with Rubens Faria piqued my interest to learn more about psychic healers. I researched these types of healings and was excitedly sharing what I found with Steve one evening. After sharing what I felt was the most amazing information, he looked at me and said, "I'm sorry, it just doesn't interest me." My heart sank. In that moment, a part of me knew we weren't going to make it. I was deeply saddened I couldn't share this part of my life with him.

Often the Fractured Phoenix will find herself alone on the spiritual path. As she learns of the connection between all, the ability to communicate with animals and to hear from beings beyond this dimension, a divide can begin between her and her more conventional partner. Some choose to stay in the relationship. Some choose to leave. Neither choice is wrong. It's a deeply personal decision each of us needs to make with love, contemplation, and integrity.

My choice came in the form of a new friend. We met at a weeklong horse clinic near my home. Lynn was staying at the horse farm where the clinic was held. We quickly became best friends. She shared my spiritual beliefs and supported my emerging work with the animals. We talked often on the phone and shared long emails about our dreams and desires. After several months of friendship from a distance, we met again for another horse clinic. This time Lynn stayed with Steve and me for the clinic. It was this weekend when I realized my feelings had changed and I was in love with my new girlfriend. Though I had known all along she was lesbian, it never occurred to me I would ever be physically attracted to a woman. It stunned me when I had these new feelings. "My God, I thought, what will this do to Steve?" The thought of leaving him was unbearable. The grief indescribable. I still loved him.

I desperately wanted Steve to share the path I had chosen. As I lay on my futon in my office one day crying, he came in. I had been listening to an uplifting talk from a Unity Minister. I told him, "I don't want to go down this path without you. Please, please, come with me." I'm certain he knew I was talking about having a spiritual life.

He said, "I'm sorry, I can't".

I went back to my therapist to explore my feelings. She told me, "Wendy, I'm certain you are not a lesbian." Perhaps, but maybe bi-sexual? I talked with a life coach and a few of my woman mentors. Interestingly, the life coach was lesbian as were two of my energy workers and the animal communicator mentor. I noticed how I had surrounded myself with other lesbians. I wondered if there was a connection.

Another piece to the puzzle came about in a friendship with my first love. He and I met in high school and dated on and off for several years until I wanted college and he wanted marriage. He married someone else, and years later, our paths crossed and we became friends again. At the time I discovered I was in love with a woman, we had been in touch and I shared with him about my feelings for Lynn. He told me he too had something to share. As it turns out, my first love was transgender; a woman trapped in a man's body. Several years later, he had sexual reassignment surgery and became a woman. The first man I fell in love with was really a woman.

One of my energy workers tried to dissuade me from continuing this friendship. She felt Steve was my Soul mate. I chose to ignore her advice. I asked for guidance. At the time, all I recognized was confirmation that this was meant to be. Each time I asked Spirit for guidance, I would interpret the message to mean leave Steve; be with this woman.

Though part of me was mesmerized by the idea of Lynn and me together, creating a business with horses, helping people through Equine Assisted Learning or something similar, another part was terrified.

As a child, I had learned to dissociate from my pain and my fear. I was ignoring my fear, as I had learned to do so well when it was actually a useful tactic. The weeks during which I was debating what to do, (yet before I said something to Steve), I could barely sleep an hour per night. My adrenaline was in complete overdrive and I was losing about a half pound of weight per day. Rather than understand this as fear that I should pay attention to, I characterized it as the "in love diet."

At one point, I asked for insight into my decision and using the animal medicine cards, pulled Coyote, the trickster. According to Sams & Carson, Medicine Cards, "Coyote refines the art of self-sabotage to sheer perfection ... Coyote takes himself so seriously at times that he cannot see the obvious; for example the steamroller that is about to roll over him ... Snooze time is over if you have pulled the Coyote medicine card. Watch out!"

I wondered if this meant leaving Steve would be a mistake. I spoke again to my wise mentor friend. "Do you think Lynn is the trickster?" I asked. "Is she conning me? Am I conning myself?" Her reply was that she was certain Lynn wasn't evil, but felt I needed to stop communications with her to get clear. I decided to tell Lynn I couldn't leave Steve. I wasn't going to go through with the divorce, and we needed to stop communicating. She begged me to not stop the communication. She cried. She said I had to remain her friend. I didn't know how to separate her feelings or energy from mine.

One of the most debilitating aspects of developing empathic abilities as a traumatized child is that you will continue to feel as if you are responsible for others' feelings until you recognize what you are doing and develop healthy boundaries. My child-self felt she must protect my friend. I couldn't let Lynn feel pain because I could not separate her from me. This isn't empathy but enmeshment. I didn't know how to honor my own feelings at the expense of someone else's, because as a child, this ability kept me safe. My child self thought she might literally die if this other person's feelings were not attended to.

Though Steve was also hurting, he never merged his energy with me as she had done. I was able to separate myself from him, but not from her. When you are in relationship with someone where you feed on each other's energy, enmeshment can happen. In psychotherapy, this dynamic is referred to as codependency. The energetic form is energy cords. I didn't understand energy cords or codependency back then. I didn't know how the cords we both were using were keeping this dynamic going.

Here is an explanation of codependency from www.Mentalhealthamerica.net *"Dysfunctional families do not acknowledge that problems exist. They don't talk about them or confront them. As a result, family members learn to repress emotions and disregard their own needs. They become 'survivors.' They develop behaviors that help them deny, ignore, or avoid difficult emotions. They detach themselves. They don't talk. They don't touch. They don't confront. They don't feel. They don't trust. The identity and emotional development of the members of a dysfunctional family are often inhibited.*

Attention and energy will focus on the family member who is ill or addicted. The codependent person typically sacrifices his or her needs to take care of a person who is sick. When co-dependents place other people's health, welfare, and safety before their own, they can lose contact with their own needs, desires, and sense of self."

I had become an expert at ignoring my own true desires and emotions.

Materialistically, my life was awesome. We had a beautiful home and had just built a new barn to finally bring my horses home. We were also beginning plans on a winter home in Arizona. It appeared I had everything. Yet I was lonely and depressed. Though Steve tried to be a loving supportive husband, the lack of emotional and spiritual intimacy, compounded with my wounded self, was more than the relationship could handle.

The divorce was fast. Ours was a clean divorce using mediation with no arguing about anything. Steve packed up everything and stored it in the garage for me. He even took the brand new horse fencing down so I would not have to do it...or so I would not be around to do it. It all came about so easily; well, at least from the standpoint of dividing property and assets.

Let me assure you there is nothing easy about leaving the man you have loved for 18 years, and still love, financial security, and a life you thought you knew.

My horses and I moved north to Lynn's ten acre farmette. As I stared in the mirror in her bathroom, I did not recognize the woman I saw. *Who are you? Where have you taken me? What have you done?* It all seemed so surreal and dreamlike. Yet here I was with a woman. Moving from one moment of bliss and passion to the deepest grief I have ever known. It occurred to me I might have developed split personalities (multiple personality disorder or dissociative identity disorder) like my oldest sister. Maybe I have been a multiple all along and this unknown personality took over, left my husband and moved 100 miles north to a rural area in a small house to be with a woman. A woman. What the hell happened? Who was this woman looking back at me in the mirror? Standing in front of the mirror I would ask, "who are you?" But the cloud of illusion that comes with new love obscured everything else.

It would be years before I began to understand how

my empathic abilities had not served me well in this regard. I would not say it was a mistake. All of our experiences have treasures. At the time I needed the support she provided. I needed someone who believed in my abilities, walked the same spiritual path, and allowed me the space to discover myself. Perhaps if I had understood the energetic cords, codependency, and my lack of boundaries operating at the time, I might have made different decisions. I do not know if I would still be with Steve today had I not left him then.

Because of your early energetic experiences, understanding energy cords and boundaries is essential to healing, taking back your power and living without encumbrances. You can learn how to manage energy cords and boundaries in Chapter 30, Energy Boundaries & Attachments.

18

A New Community

IN THIS RURAL AREA of central Wisconsin, I found many Soul Sisters who would become family to me. In my previous community, I had two close friends and two sisters. As I rose from the ashes, our connection faltered. Though I still had a deep love for my friends and sisters, as my experiences and beliefs changed, so too did our relationships. I had no idea how desperately I longed for the deep loving connections and understanding I discovered in my new home. It's hard to know what you are missing when you've never experienced it.

In just a couple of years, I had developed deep friendships with two groups of women. One group of us would meet every week for coffee to share, laugh, and cry together. We held each other up through divorce, career changes, breast cancer, and more. And we celebrated, new adopted children, grand children, marriages, new businesses, and promotions. Our weekly meetings allowed me to be supported in a way I hadn't experienced with other women prior to this.

The other group of women I call my Soul Sisters. We gather for dancing, for full and new moons, and for many rituals to open our hearts and bring forth the best we can be. Each woman has wisdom to share and collectively, we are a force of wise and powerful women. From January to April, one of these women guides a three month women's circle that sustains me through each long Wisconsin winter. As the weather warms, we gather for local music, dancing, and swimming in the clear waters of the nearby lakes.

There is nothing more powerful and healing than being surrounded by like-minded friends who love you unconditionally. My new sisters helped me learn about compassion for myself and for others. They've supported my dreams as I have theirs. There is a sacred bond we share as women. We support each other with a fierceness exceeded only by its gentleness. Having this support is essential to healing your fractures. Find your tribe. Embrace them. Love them. Play with them often. Dance to the moonlight, sing, chant, and drum together.

19

Embracing My Healing Abilities

RUBENS FARIA NEVER RETURNED to Wisconsin. I searched online for him for years, yet never found any way to contact him. Not finding him haunted me. He wasn't finished with me. There was more healing I needed. Even though I was doing the work I loved, my fractures were not completely mended. Doubts and shame crept into my everyday life in sinister ways. Depression and anxiety filtered in like smoke through a leaky window. How could I ever complete my healing?

This question haunted me for years. How could I find him to complete my healing? Was there someone else who could help? Who could help me bring freedom out of my brokenness? Who could turn my darkness into light? Someone needed to fix me. Then I heard about *John of God*.

About eight years after Rubens, some friends and I attended a talk about John of God. The young man who spoke with us had taken several trips to see John of God and was now escorting others as a guide. I was excited about the possibility of going to Brazil to see him and experience what I felt would be a heart-opening experience. I didn't have any physical issues to speak of, but I had the sense maybe he could finish what Rubens Faria began. Maybe he could fix me.

The guide shared with us the specifics of a trip and mentioned the airport we would need to fly into. The next day as I was costing out the trip, I could not remember the name of the airport. I said out loud, "I need to know the name of the airport." At the same time I could see a storm brewing out to the west. The clouds looked menacing so I turned on the TV to check the weather. Just as the sound from the TV came on the newscaster said "today in Brasilia"...which was the name of the airport I needed. This was a good sign. I contacted the guide and let him know I wanted to go with him on his next trip.

The next week, one of my friends who had gone with me to the talk on John of God, gave me the book, John of God. "I've had this for a while and noticed it today and knew right away I needed to give it to you." As soon as I had a free moment, I began to read about John of God.

João Teixeira de Faria , known as John of God, has been offering healing to people from all over the world at what is known as the Casa de Dom Inacio de Loyola in Abadiania, Goias, Brazil for over forty years. He is an unconscious medium who channels entities that do the healing. "I do not cure anybody. God heals, and in his infinite goodness permits the Entities to heal and console my brothers. I am merely an instrument in God's divine hands." – John of God.

I read the book and learned about the three entities: Dr Augusto de Almeida, Dr Oswaldo Cruz, and the spiritual patron of the clinic, Saint Ignatius de Loyola.

There is a room filled with crutches, walkers and wheelchairs discarded by people who found they no longer needed them after their healing sessions. Although John of God is quick to point out not all will heal from their physical ailments, spiritual healing is quite common.

Patients all dressed in white, line up in a large room, waiting to have just moments with John of God. Often they are then told to go spend several hours in meditation in the "channel" room. Here, many dedicated healers spend the day holding the energy and meditating for the healing of others.

I started to imagine what it would feel like to be in the channel room. I remembered the overwhelming bliss I felt in the chapel at the Miracles Healing Center as I waited to see Rubens Faria. I wanted that experience again. I wanted the peace back. I wanted to feel right about my life.

As I thought about the meditation room I began to sense the peace. I felt the energy *as if I were there,* all from the comfort of my sunroom couch. The warmth of the energy grew and I felt a presence with me. This tingly knowing came over me. Someone was here. John of God's Spirit helper came to me. I was aware Saint Ignatius de Loyola was with me. I could feel him working in my energy body. I welcomed him and relaxed into the assistance he was providing. He began talking to me. He told me it was not necessary for me to travel to John of God for healing. If I chose to, seeking out John of God was fine. But all I needed was to invite him in with a pure heart and the healing would take place.

Really? It was hard not to question the idea I could facilitate my own healing. It was hard not to think I was making this all up. Who am I to call in a special entity who works with John of God? Who am I to receive this energy?

We are raised in a culture that tells us to always look outside of ourselves for answers. As young children we are told to listen to our elders, to obey, and not question. Our social system does not support the idea that we have answers within ourselves, but rather, that we are to hand over control to the "authority" or "expert." We are taught powerlessness from a very early age.

Even many of the spiritual "new age" culture would suggest I need to go to someone special, someone trained to receive healing. They would warn me not to let these other unknown spirits into my energy field. I could hear a healer I know telling me that calling in these spirits could be dangerous without proper training and attunements. I have never believed this. This idea is a hierarchical view of energy abilities. The idea we need some special training seems too much like the other systems of our power-controlled, patriarchal society.

As I sat on my comfortable couch, I could feel Saint Ignatius De Loyola in my energy body. I could feel energy moving around. I felt warm breezes inside the room with no windows open. An energy tornado swirled around me, picking up everything in its path, twisting me and pulling the old studs of fear, guilt and anger out of my foundation. A vortex of healing swept over me and I landed gently in a place of peace.

I was reminded of the lesson I had been learning for years. It was the lesson to trust my own knowing. Here's how my learning often happened. First, I worried about some aspect of my life. I would stew and wonder what I should do. Then I would reach out to someone I felt could help me. I would ask for their insight. Invariably the advice would not meet my needs. The answer was with me all along. I only needed to get quiet and hear the still voice inside. I would remember this for a while until something else came along that scared me or made me unsettled. I was aware of this dynamic. I would say to God or whoever is orchestrating this all…"I get it; I'm to stop looking outside myself for the answers." Eventually, I came to realize when I needed information I didn't have, I could ask for clarity, and people would show up in my life with answers.

We are given access to all the information we might need. The answers we need can come from listening within or they can come in the comment of a stranger, a book that falls off the shelf or from the new person your friend just knew you should meet. To this day, I still sometimes call on Saint Ignatius de Loyola for healing and feel his presence. All clarity requires is that we ask. Ask and ye shall receive. How cool is that?!

20

Becoming the Teacher

AFTER A COUPLE OF YEARS communicating and facilitating animal healing full-time, I began to teach animal communication and animal aromatherapy. With an education degree and years facilitating workshops in business and marketing-related topics, teaching came naturally. I remember the joy I felt after teaching my first animal communication class. I was thrilled to have so much fun and get paid. It was such a different feeling than my previous jobs where I came to dread the work.

After teaching animal communication for about two years, I noticed a trend. The students who were exceptionally gifted had experienced difficult childhoods and were energetically sensitive.

I realized those who have experienced difficult childhoods tend to be Highly Sensitive Empaths (HSE), a term I created to describe a person who feels energy from other people, animals, spirits, and even plants. We walk in the world with our energy field reaching out to others and absorbing energy. We don't do this consciously; it's how we are. Our *energy field* is more sensitive and often more expansive. We are more intuitive as a result because we are more in tune to the energy of the world. Since our world is composed completely of energy, we are more aware of what is happening around us if we are aware of our sensitivity.

HSEs are spiritual and creative by nature. We feel more and think more deeply than others. We are generally considered "seekers."

There are a few terms that are similar but not the same. They are *empath, highly sensitive person,* and *a sensitive.* Each of these is different and yet one person can have all of these traits.

An *Empath* is someone who can literally feel the emotions and physical feelings of other humans, animals, and all life. Many of us are familiar with the character Deanna Troi of *Star Trek: The Next Generation*, who is portrayed as an empath. She has the ability to feel others' emotions. True empaths can also feel physical feelings from others.

Here's an example from my experience. One morning, while working in a business with my sister, I walked into the building (where she was in the basement loading a kiln with pottery) when all of a sudden, I noticed very painful menstrual cramps. I was surprised as it wasn't time for me to have cramps. After about ten minutes my sister came up from the kiln room and announced she had very bad cramps. "Oh these are yours," I said. Once I realized I was experiencing her pain, I was able to let it go just as easily. This was not always true. It was something I learned through trial and error. Until you learn how to manage the empathy, you are subject to physical and emotional feelings that don't belong to you.

A *Highly Sensitive Person* (HSP) as defined by Dr. Elaine Aron, is someone whose brain processes information differently than others. They are very observant of their surroundings, and therefore, can be overwhelmed by the amount of information they take in. HSPs are born this way and are often described as introverts. Some of the traits attributed to a highly sensitive person include sensitivity to loud noises, bright lights, strong smells, are easily overwhelmed, tend to avoid crowds and violent or scary movies, and often need to withdraw from others. While a Highly Sensitive Empath does process information through their brain like a HSP, how they use their energy field differs from others. Of course, you can be both!

Another term often used in the "new age" world, is "sensitive." Someone is said to be a "sensitive" if they readily pick up on Spirits, beings in other dimensions and psychic information. A highly sensitive empath may or may not naturally be a "sensitive." Picking up other information is a skill that can be learned. It can come as a result of practice with meditation or other exercises that train you to become aware of dimensions beyond the three dimensional world which we typically experience. It is ultimately under your control.

The Highly Sensitive Empath is an empath with other intuitive abilities, such as communicating with animals and an energy field capable of channeling large amounts of energy for the purpose of healing oneself or another. We generally have traits of a Highly Sensitive person as well.

Some people were simply born this way. Others can be born this way, but they may also hyper-develop this sensitivity through early childhood experiences of trauma, including physical, sexual, emotional or ritual abuse; illness; premature birth; death of a parent or sibling; trauma while in the womb; and mental illness in the family. These challenging experiences caused us to feel unsafe in the world and continually "send" our energy to the people and situations surrounding us. We did this to "read them" or discover their emotional state. We often used this information to make decisions about how to keep ourselves safe. As part of this process, we often created an attachment or "energy cord" of our energy to theirs. It was an unconscious coping and survival mechanism that became a way of being.

Through the experience of trauma, we are cracked open. Because we understand how it feels to be scared, in physical and/or emotional pain, we choose not to inflict this on others, and because we learned to unconsciously "feel" others, we can literally feel their pain. Thus, our pain often instills deep compassion and empathy. Many of us learn how to channel this sensitivity into helping ourselves and others through healing and intuitive abilities.

The first step in learning how to channel our sensitivity is awareness. As we become more familiar with how our own energy body feels, we can begin to sense when our energy field is being influenced by another.

When we are not aware of our sensitivity, we can easily feel overwhelmed by large crowds, loud noises, angry voices and cluttered rooms (stuff has energy... more stuff equals more energy). We often unconsciously absorb other people's or animals energies into our own, contributing to anxiety, depression, fatigue and illness. Even when we have this awareness, we can feel overwhelmed. Once we learn how to manage our energy by changing our energy patterns and pathways, we can eliminate a great deal of overwhelm through awareness and practices of self care.

Because we live in a multi-dimensional world,

many of us also feel energies that reside in dimensions beyond the three dimensions of physicality. These "energies" can come from animals or people who have left their physical body, more commonly referred to as "spirits." They can also come from plants, trees and non-earthly beings. This sensitivity allows us to feel, hear, or see these spirits or "energies." Each person is different in his or her sensitivity.

HSEs sometimes experience premonitions. These can come in the form of a knowing, a dream, or a waking vision. This happens because of our open connection to energy, the universal consciousness where all information and knowing resides. For us, the veil between the dimensions is very thin.

I had a dream about a year before I met Lynn, who would become my partner for ten years. In the dream, I had left Steve for a woman. I was mad at him because he didn't stop me from leaving. When I awoke from the dream, I told Steve I was mad at him because he let me leave him for a woman. We laughed about it in the way we always did when I presented my dreams to him as reality and he would remind me they were just dreams. When I remembered the dream after leaving Steve, I realized it was a premonition. I wondered why I didn't remember it until after I had left.

21

Finding the Link

My work with animals attracted many women who experienced early childhood trauma. I found survivors often feel connected to animals. For some of us, animals were the only beings that felt safe. Survivors share traits we often associate more with animals than humans. Like animals, we are energetically sensitive and in tune with nature. Energetic sensitivity is part of an animal's instinctual nature. They are never taught to ignore their energetic senses. It's how they survive in the world. We feel the world around us as the animals do. For many, an animal's energy feels more comfortable than the energy of people. Animals who need a home or an understanding human find us. They can tell we are more sensitive and more compassionate. It is not uncommon to have a butterfly or dragonfly land on us and stay for a while. Squirrels, rabbits, birds, and deer are often comfortable coming close to us. Injured wild birds and animals seek us out. They can sense from our energy field that we have the capacity to communicate with them, and they trust us.

In their book, *Healing Developmental Trauma, How Early Trauma Affects Self-Regulation, Self-Image, and the Capacity for Relationship*, Laurence Heller, PhD and Aline LaPierre, PsyD, delineate five adaptive survival styles based on the onset age and type of trauma experienced by children. One style, "Connection" has a subset known as the "Spiritualizing Subtype." Those who direct their coping skills in this manner tend to connect with animals and leave their bodies often. As they explain: *"These subtypes are prone to spiritualizing their experience. As a result of either early shock or relational trauma, they did not feel welcomed into the world and grew up believing that the world is a cold, loveless place. Because other humans are often experienced as threats, many individuals with this subtype search for spiritual connection, are more comfortable in nature and with animals, and feel more connected to God than to other human beings. To make sense of the pain in their lives, they often become spiritual seekers, trying to convince themselves that someone loves them; if people do not, then God must.*

These individuals are often sensitive in both positive and negative ways. Having never embodied, they have access to energetic levels of information to which less traumatized people are not as sensitive; they can be quite psychic and energetically attuned to people, animals and the environment and can feel confluent and invaded by other people's emotions. They are also unable to filter environmental stimuli - they are sensitive to light, sound, pollution, electromagnetic waves, touch, etc.; therefore they often struggle with environmental sensitivities."

If we use spiritualism as an escape from this world, we will remain overly sensitive and hostage to the energies around us. As we go through the healing process, which includes awareness of how our early experiences have affected how we view the world, how our nervous system and physical body have been changed as a result, and how it changes our relationships with others and ourselves, then we can learn to live in our body and connect to other people with an open heart. Only when we are able to connect authentically with others and accept ourselves as we are will we able to heal completely. We also heal by living energetically within our body using grounding as a means to help us stay in the body.

While Heller and LaPierre see the Spiritual Subset as a coping mechanism, I see it from a slightly different perspective. I agree that it is a coping mechanism, but I also believe it's possible that our Souls chose our early life experiences because it would invoke our quest for a spiritual connection and gift us with this sensitivity. Our challenge is to heal the fractures from our wounding so that we can use the gifts of our broken childhood to help others heal, as our Souls may have intended.

Part 2

Regaining Control of Your Energy

"As information processing machines, our ability to process data about the external world begins at the level of sensory perception. Although most of us are rarely aware of it, our sensory receptors are designed to detect information at the energy level. Because everything around us... the air we breathe even the materials we build with... are composed of spinning and vibrating atomic particles, you and I are literally swimming in a turbulent sea of electromagnetic fields. We are part of it. We are enveloped in it and through our sensory apparatus we experience WHAT IS".

—Jill Bolte Taylor, *My Stroke of Insight*

22

Understanding Energy & Your Auric Field

As a child, sending out my energy to "feel" others and ascertain safety was completely unconscious. I didn't understand energy. I was clueless about what my own energy body felt like. As I began working with animals and learning about energy through my own experiences, classes, and books, I became familiar with how my energy felt without attachments from others.

As you begin to understand how energy works, it will help you to connect with animals (and guides, Spirits, plants, etc.) and allow you to experience more ease. You can find more joy, love, and connection. When you become familiar with your energy body, you can more easily identify what is not "yours." You can learn to be responsible with your energy body and to manage other energy (from people, places, etc.) that can be draining. You can also learn to allow universal energy to flow more easily through you. When energy flows through without obstruction, your energetic vibration becomes a higher frequency. This, in turn, creates more joy and abundant health. Higher vibrations equal emotions of gratitude, love, and joy as well as a heightened immune system and overall good health. Lower vibrations equal emotions of fear, guilt, powerlessness, etc. Many of the current books on energy will recommend shielding or other ways of "protecting" yourself from outside energies. The skilled Fractured Phoenix knows she can flow with all of the energy present, while keeping other energies from adhering to her. Specific techniques are offered later in the book.

Your energy body is a multilayered electromagnetic field known as the auric field. It is the first place you meet the world. Your auric field typically extends about two to three feet out from your body in a cocoon-like dimension. It extends above and below your body as well. There are seven layers within this field, each layer vibrating at a higher level the further you get from the body. For the exercises you will be learning in this book, knowledge of each layer is not necessary.

Our body also contains hundreds of "points" of concentrated energy. The system of acupuncture is based on these energy points. According to Eastern tradition, there are seven major energy "centers", commonly referred to as "chakras." "Chakra" is a Sanskrit word meaning "wheel." The energy centers can be viewed as spinning wheels of energy, each having an associated color. Through these energy centers we take in, process and release the energy or life force known as Chi or Prana.

Each chakra corresponds to specific aspects of our consciousness and physical body with their own characteristics and functions. Together, they work as a synergistic system through which body, mind, and spirit interact. When one or more of the energy centers are blocked, it can manifest in physical, emotional, and spiritual issues. Clearing these energy centers through regular meditation (like the Energy Mastery meditation), sound, movement, or receiving energy work connects the physical body with the spiritual body, thus bringing about wholeness.

The First Chakra, the root chakra, is located at the base of the spine, and is a vibrant red color. This is the chakra of manifestation and is associated with grounding, survival, and beginnings. This is the chakra we use to ground our energy deep into the earth. It affects prosperity and feeling safe in the world. As the chakra of survival, it can be weakened by early life trauma. Therefore, focusing on keeping this chakra vibrant and balanced is important. If you experience fear, anxiety or feel unsafe, try wearing the color red, spending more time in nature, and visualizing a vibrant red lotus flower at the base of your spine. When fear arises, say to yourself, "I am safe, I am loved, I am whole." Of course, if you experience consistent fear and anxiety, seek the help of a trauma professional.

The Second Chakra is known as the sacral chakra and is orange in color. It is located in the lower abdomen, centered between the navel and the genitals and impacts creativity, emotion, pleasure, and sexuality. Because it is associated with empathy, it is important to the Highly Sensitive Empath. For us, it will be important to keep this chakra balanced so we are not overcome by emotions we pick up from others. Sometimes referred to as the "seat of life," this chakra is also known in the martial arts as the "Hara", the center of your energy field. When you are feeling ungrounded or anxious, focus your attention two inches below your belly button and imagine your energy concentrating at this point. This will help stabilize and center you. This technique works especially well when working with horses or needing to feel strong and balanced.

The Third Chakra is the solar plexus chakra and is yellow in color. It is located at the navel and deals with self-esteem, energy, will, power, and autonomy. It is the place of information or worldly knowledge. Those who experienced early life trauma often have a weakened solar plexus chakra, leading them to feel powerless. Be mindful as you go through your energy cord exercises to note who might be attached to you at this chakra. When this chakra is weakened, it is an invitation to others who need energy (specifically power) to attach to you at this point. Staying alert to this possibility will help you eliminate attachments. Keeping this chakra balanced will help avoid attachments.

The Fourth Chakra is the heart chakra and is emerald green in color. It is located in the heart area and regulates balance, love, compassion, healing, and unity. The heart is the intersection point between the "lower" earth chakras and the "higher" spiritual chakras. When the heart chakra is beginning to open, Dr. Motoyama indicates in his book, *Theories of the Chakras,* that there is often pain in the front of the chest or irregular function of the heart, like an accelerated pulse. Keeping this chakra open, balanced, and activated is vital to keeping others' energy from attaching to you. When your heart chakra is open, energy flows freely through you rather than attaching to you. An open heart chakra is also essential to energy healing and animal communication abilities.

The Fifth Chakra is the throat chakra and is sky blue in color. It is located in the throat area, and is the vortex of sound, vibration, and communication. It is this energy center that allows us to speak our truth. For those of us who experienced trauma, it is not unusual for us to struggle to speak our truth. Often we were threatened to keep silent, creating blockages in this chakra. Thyroid or other issues of the throat can indicate a closed throat chakra.

The Sixth Chakra is the third eye chakra and is a dark indigo blue in color. It is located between the eyebrows and supports intuition, imagination, visualization, clairvoyance, and vision. Many believe this chakra is connected with the pineal gland and is the "seat of the Soul." It vibrates at a higher frequency than sound. The third eye's vibration is that of light and is typically open for most survivors unless they have shut it down due to overwhelm from too much information coming through the third eye.

The Seventh Chakra is the crown chakra and is violet or white in color. It is located above the head and is the center of consciousness and divine connection. It has been called the "seat of enlightenment." Many survivors will energetically live out of this chakra. Rather than containing all of their energy fully within their body, they will maintain the mass of their energy within this chakra. This is not useful and is why embodied living and grounding is so important to the survivor and highly sensitive empath.

Clearing Chakras involves releasing negative thoughts or dark energy from our chakras and then balancing the chakras by enlarging them so they are all the same size. Visualize each chakra swirling with brilliant color within your body. Glen Velez, the creator of "Rhythms of the Chakras, Drumming for the Body's Energy Centers" has a site that offers a sample of his compositions that can heal all the chakras.

Practicing the Energy Mastery meditation available at www.wendywolfe.com, will teach you how to enhance your energy field by disengaging from others, clearing what isn't yours, and grounding your energy. Through this process, you can protect yourself by allowing other energy to flow through you without clinging, concentrate your energy near your Sacral or Hara chakra, and anchor to the powerful energy of Mother Earth.

23

Controlling Your Auric Field

IN 2004, I WAS LEARNING craniosacral therapy for horses at a workshop. Our instructor, a woman sensitive to energy, asked that as she demonstrated some techniques for us, we not "join" her energetically. We were to keep our energy to ourselves. She did not want others' energy interfering with the work she was doing. The horse she was demonstrating on was my big black Tennessee Walking Horse, Indy. As soon as she began working on Indy, my energy...and the other students' energy joined her. She let us know she felt our energy (in a terse scolding fashion) but she didn't tell us how not to send our energy. I was embarrassed I had done exactly what she asked us not to do. I didn't even know how I had done it, except that I was focusing my attention on Indy.

As I thought about this, I realized my energy followed my attention…where your attention goes your energy follows. I knew when I intentionally sent my energy to an animal to communicate with it, the energy followed. But now I realized, *if I wasn't paying attention, my thoughts alone would send my energy off to another place or being.*

It was a light bulb moment, a clear "aha" for me. I decided to use my thoughts to control the situation. I imagined myself in a Plexiglas tube. The tube was open on the top and bottom so energy from the earth and Universe could still flow to me but my energy would not leave the tube. Because it was clear, I could be completely aware of all happening around me. Once I did this, the teacher was satisfied and didn't mention the intruding energy again.

From this experience I figured out how to withdraw my energy and still observe what she was doing for the remainder of the course. I also learned how subtle the thoughts can be which send our energy elsewhere.

A client's experience demonstrates how our energy follows our attention. Sitting in my office, I received a call from a woman in panic…literally. She was in the midst of a panic attack and called me for help. Sara was out west enjoying a great conference with like-minded people. She was outside with her group when they all noticed a large herd of elk crossing through a field, making their way toward a road. Sara grabbed her camera and set it up on a tripod to capture the moment. For most of us, watching a herd of elk move across a field is not a daily occurrence. As she looked through the camera lens, she discovered a cow (female elk) separated from the herd. She looked right into the eyes of this cow and realized she had large cataracts on her eyes and was probably nearly blind. She could sense and feel the panic of this cow. And within moments, she found herself in the midst of a full blown panic attack.

Some of the herd waited for this cow and she eventually was able to get back to the others in the herd.

But for Sara, the panic was still there. She didn't know how to release her panic, so she called me. As she explained to me what had transpired, I immediately understood what happened to her. I talked her through a simple exercise to ground her energy and the feelings of panic and overwhelming fear subsided. She was able to disconnect her energy from the cow and the energy of panic left.

In her book, *Finding Your Way in a Wild New World*, Martha Beck recounts a similar experience she had in the wilds of Africa. She witnessed the death of a young gazelle and as she explains it, she continued to feel the emotions of the gazelles that occurred in the last moments of the young one's life for a couple of days. Too bad she didn't have my phone number ;-) ... although I suspect Martha knows a few techniques herself.

Some scientists believe our thoughts are actually energy. Not all are in agreement as it has yet been unable to be proven. What we do know is our thoughts and our intentions direct and influence our energy or auric field. Changing our thoughts can change what happens with our energy field. Positive loving thoughts will raise our own energy vibration just as thoughts of anger and grief will lower the vibration.

Because our thoughts "send" our energy to different places, people and things, when you think of someone, your energy goes to them and makes a connection. Usually, when you stop thinking of the person, your energy leaves them. However, when there is strong emotion attached to the thought, your energetic connection becomes stronger. In some cases, this connection becomes an attachment, or "energy cord." Of course this means that others' energy can become attached to you as well, merely from them thinking of you with a certain level of emotion.

If you need something from them, i.e., their approval, love, some action, your attachment will likely be pulling energy from them. Some refer to this as "stealing energy" though it is unconscious. More detail is provided on energy exchanges in "Discovering Energy Habits."

It may be hard to believe that you can control your

energy with thoughts and intention, yet there are studies which demonstrate how our intention and thoughts can even change physical matter.

24

The Power of Intention

THE INSTITUTE OF HEARTMATH in Boulder Creek, California, conducted studies to observe the effect that intention (thoughts) has on physical matter, specifically, DNA. The results were nothing less than astounding. With thoughts and intention, people were able to measurably alter DNA in another location.

The most important thing to understand is that to change physical matter in a way that we want, we need to be in what HeartMath refers to as Heart Coherence. I first learned of this at a workshop with author Gregg Braden. As Heart Coherence was described, I realized he was describing the same process I use to teach others to communicate with animals. Heart Coherence is a measurable state of the heart and can be generated by creating an overwhelming sense of love and gratitude.

Here's a summary of the findings in a nutshell. *"All individuals capable of generating high ECG coherence ratios (heart coherence) could alter the conformation of DNA according to their intention. Intending to unwind or wind the DNA produced increases or decreases in the UV absorption peak at 260 nm. Untrained individuals, <u>who were not able to sustain feelings of love,</u> showed low ratios of ECG coherence and were unable to intentionally alter the conformation of DNA."* (underline author's addition.)[1]

In a well-structured scientific study, these results demonstrate that when in a state of Heart Coherence, participants are able to alter DNA with their thoughts.

Seriously, think about this.

Your thoughts and heart can change physical matter. This is huge.

Those who were more proficient at the *Heart Coherence* state were able to have more effect on the specific strands of DNA. With their intention and thoughts, they loosened and tightened strands of DNA. In some cases the DNA was in another location a half mile away. The founder of HeartMath, Doc Childre, when presented with three strands of DNA in one vessel was able to tighten one, loosen another and leave the third one alone.

In my experience, those who have experienced early childhood trauma have a greater capacity to go into and maintain a state of Heart Coherence. While I have no scientific evidence, I have a theory. When a heart is broken open repeatedly, the result can be a more open, loving and receptive heart. When we tear certain fibers in our muscles, the process of repairing the muscle builds stronger, larger muscles. Our heart is a muscle. Perhaps the more it is broken, the stronger it becomes. This would explain the increased ability to stay in a place of love and gratitude which allows us to maintain Heart Coherence.

[1] *Modulation of DNA Conformation by Heart-Focused Intention – McCraty, Atkinson, Tomasino, 2003 HeartMath Research Center, Institute of HeartMath, Publication No. 03-008. Boulder Creek, CA, 2003*

25

The Fractured Phoenix on Autopilot

IN HIS BOOK, *Complex PTSD, From Surviving to Thriving,* Pete Walker observes how the desire to survive instills certain behaviors with his clients. He sees this through the eyes of psychotherapy and I see it through energy, although I believe we are observing the same phenomenon. *"Many...survived by constantly focusing their awareness on their parents to figure out what was needed to appease them. Some became almost psychic in their ability to read their parent's minds and expectations.....Survivors now need to deconstruct this habit by working to stay more inside their own experience without constantly projecting their attention outward to read others."* Because of my experience with my energy following my thoughts and emotions, I see this attachment to the parent energetically.

When we are not conscious of our energy, we will use it in the way we learned in our early childhood, which often means dispersing out to "read" other people. This can result in us taking on other people's energy like a sponge. When we take on others' energy, we become overwhelmed with feelings that are not our own. It can drag us down and eventually cause physical and emotional illness.

We have created patterns or pathways with our energy bodies that are operating unconsciously. I first made this connection while learning about new brain research.

While studying the brain, scientists have discovered that early experiences in our lives create certain neural pathways. This means that under certain circumstances, our brains respond in the same way they did when we were children. These pathways become habitual thought patterns, which then can become beliefs or "stories" we tell ourselves. Generally, our "stories" aren't true (at least not anymore) but they continue to influence our decisions and reactions in life. They are comfortable...it is what we know, even when they sometimes cause misery. A few examples of "stories" are: I always get sick in the winter, I'm not good at socializing, or I never have time to do what I want for me.

Neuroscientists have discovered that we can *reprogram* these pathways by being observant of our thoughts and "course correcting" the thoughts as they come up. Byron Katie's "The Work" is a classic example of examining our thoughts and asking key questions to ascertain their validity. (If you aren't familiar with her work, I recommend you check it out...she has several books).

Those who experienced trauma use a similar action with their energy field. Early in life we send our energy out to read other people. We do this to sense the emotions of others as a way of protecting ourselves by being able to get out of the way of other dangerous emotions. Over the years, our energy does this unconsciously; we create energy pathways that are on autopilot.

When we are young children, we want to please our parents. After all, we are completely dependent upon them and need their love. We are sensitive to their energy and emotions. When our parents are not happy (regardless of why), we unconsciously connect our energy to them because we want them to be happy. Our desire for them to be happy while connected to their energy caused us to unknowingly take on their negative energy in an attempt to change their emotional state. This is especially true if we have experienced abuse when they are not happy. Eventually we create a pattern of absorbing the energy of others we care about (children, partners, friends, animals, clients). It becomes an "energy pathway" that is not helping us or them.

It is the nature of highly sensitive empaths to care deeply about others and to have a strong desire for peace among people. Unknowingly, we have turned this desire into an energetic pattern which ends up depleting our energy. The good news is we can change this. Just as scientists have discovered that we can change our neural patterns and pathways, we can change our energy patterns.

_26_

Discovering Energy Habits

AT MY SECOND CRANIOSACRAL for horses training workshop, I discovered how I unconsciously shrink my energy to become "invisible" when feeling threatened. The instructor of this course could be stern. It wasn't unusual for her students to cry in the first few days of working with her. My first workshop experience made me apprehensive, but I wanted to learn more, since despite her attitude, she was very knowledgeable. Because of my apprehension, I unconsciously wanted my energy out of her space.

We began an exercise where she had us close our eyes, and then she selected a partner for each of us, and moved us so we were standing in front of each other. Because our eyes were closed, we didn't know who we were with. She then instructed us to sense the energy of the person in front of us. She had paired me with a woman who was an experienced energy worker and someone who had become my friend. After spending a few minutes to sense each other, we were instructed to open our eyes and share with each other what we sensed. When we opened our eyes and talked, she shared with me she didn't think anyone was there. She couldn't feel me at all. That's when I realized that I pulled my energy in so far, I had become "invisible." I did it automatically and unconsciously to protect myself from the teacher. I knew this technique wasn't going to serve me in this situation, so at our next break I went outside, sat on the ground and reinforced my root chakra by visualizing roots going deep into the earth. I did this continually for the week of the workshop and it worked. The teacher started responding more positively to me.

I've found with my clients that this is a common defense mechanism we used as children to make our energy so small we wouldn't be noticed. Instead of sending our energy out to feel others, at times we found it more useful to pull our energy in so far, people wouldn't notice us. We learned to become invisible. We often still do this as adults when we feel threatened emotionally or otherwise. Shrinking our energy in this way is disempowering. It no longer serves us.

It wouldn't surprise me if you've been invisible too.

—You're in a store and no one helps you.

—You raise your hand in a group only to be continually ignored.

—You talk to your partner and it's as if they don't even hear you.

Our first reaction in these situations is to blame the other. While it may be true they aren't completely present, the ability to shift the situation and change *them* lies within *you*.

Shrinking our energy into invisibility can be useful at times. We do it when we are young and don't want to draw attention to ourselves. The problem is when you aren't aware of your energy, being invisible can hamper success in many areas of your life.

Imagine you're feeling intimidated by your new boss, which triggers an old feeling of insecurity and (as if on autopilot) you pull your energy in before the big meeting. You've just unconsciously diminished your ability to be seen, heard, and respected. You also make it more difficult to be your amazing, authentic self.

Maybe you need to have a difficult conversation with your teenage daughter. You feel anxious and uncertain. Resorting to old, *unconscious* energy habits, you pull your energy in. When you meet with your daughter she is unresponsive or irritable. What you don't realize...and what she doesn't understand consciously, is when your energy is pulled in, she senses you aren't really there, that you don't care because a part of you is missing.

This unconscious energy communication can be powerful.

When you take the opportunity to shore up your energy before you meet, I guarantee the results will be different.

Being invisible affects our relationships with people and animals, reduces our "power" in the world, and allows others to dominate when it happens unconsciously.

Being invisible is a SUPER power when used strategically. Sometimes not drawing attention is *exactly* what you want. The key is awareness of your current energy field and how to manage it.

Several years after the workshop incident, I was standing alone at a counter to order dinner while the attendant was back in the kitchen. A few minutes later, two young women walked up to the counter and stood alongside me, checking out the menu. When the attendant came out from the kitchen, he looked at the two women and asked for their order. Without hesitation, they proceeded to give him their order as if they had no clue I was there first. I looked at them and realized *"I am invisible."* Okay, not invisible enough to commit a crime and get away with it, but I hadn't registered on their radar at all.

My first reaction was to feel slighted, but then realized that this had much more to do with my energy than their rudeness. As I joined my friends I said, "I've shrunk my energy so far inside, I'm invisible." The reason was clear. For two weeks I had been dealing with health issues and had unconsciously pulled my energy back. Quickly, while sitting with my friends, I internally ran an energy routine to ground and expand my energy. The energy routine I use is an abbreviated version of the Energy Meditation offered for free on my website. Later that evening, I stopped at a store to pick up a few things. At the check-out, the clerk and I connected with our eyes and smiles. We had a genuine conversation and I knew all was well with my energy.

Techniques for Energy Awareness

THE FIRST STEP IN CHANGING our energy habits is awareness. We can become familiar with how our own energy body feels from being present and paying attention. Being present is a rare occurrence for most people. We walk through our day, living in our heads, thinking about the past or the future. We worry and fret. We spend hours on social media, watching TV, or playing mindless games to numb ourselves. We neglect being in the present moment.

In my Fractured Phoenix Empowerment Classes, I teach a process called "Checking In". It's a simple process to bring you into the present moment by simply bringing your awareness into your body and engaging all of your senses. Here's how to "Check In".

Take a moment to feel into your body and notice all the sensations present. Feel your seat in the chair, feet on the floor, maybe an ache somewhere. Are there emotions present you had been distancing yourself from? Listen to all the sounds. Really pay attention to what you hear: a furnace blower, a car horn outside, the tick of the clock. Truly see through your eyes. Notice all the minute details in the area surrounding you. When you take a moment to check into all of your senses, you come into the present moment and into your body. You literally bring your energy back into your body with your attention to your body and intention to bring in your energy. It happens automatically. As soon as you feel your mind drifting, come back to noticing your body and all of your senses.

As you check into the present moment, you become aware of how your energy feels. Over time, you will begin to notice when your energy feels "off." When perhaps, all of what you feel isn't only yours. This awareness then allows you to question if you've picked up feelings from someone else. You can identify what is and isn't yours, and then release what isn't yours and move forward. Make a practice of "Checking In" several times a day. If you need a reminder, you can download an app to help you. I use the Mindful Bell app which I can set at any time interval I want. A soothing chime sounds and reminds me to "check in."

Being in the present moment (Checking In) is the

first step in "grounding." To "ground" means having your energy body fully embodied with your physical body and connected with the energy of the earth. Here's a quick method to ground you. Begin by bringing your attention to the present moment and feeling into your body. Take in a few deep breaths and visualize all your "energy" returning to you through your breath. See all your energy contained within a few feet around you, much like an egg. Next, imagine you have roots growing out of your feet that go deep into the earth ... they can go all the way to the earth's core and feel them wrap around the core to anchor you. Now, feel your energy return from the earth, traveling up those roots through your feet and legs coming to rest just below your navel at your Sacral or Hara chakra. This quick process brings your energy back to you, connects you to the energy of the earth, and centers you. Use this technique anytime you feel scattered, frightened, confused, or off balance.

Caution: If at any time during your Checking In process you feel uncomfortable, that is your breath speeds up, your muscles tighten, you notice intrusive thoughts or any other uncomfortable sensation, bring your attention back to the room. This could indicate you are in a hyper-vigilant state and seeking the help of a trauma professional is recommended.

28

Recognizing & Shifting Harmful Energy Habits

As Fractured Phoenixes, there are a few habits we may have acquired as coping mechanisms which served us at some point, but now are problematic. These habits can weaken us energetically and ultimately, physically. Following are the three most common.

#1 Leaving Your Body: As was shared earlier, this is an unconscious coping mechanism for those who experienced early trauma. This early life coping skill has become a habit which can be triggered when overwhelmed by life, engaging in excessive spiritual practice without physical activity, or experiencing pain. We allow our energy to float above us and essentially live out of our top two chakras. Unfortunately, this is one of the most detrimental habits. When your energy is floating about, you will pick up others' negative energy. Because you are not grounded in this state, lower vibration energy sticks to you like Velcro.

The Shift: Consciously bring all of your energy into your body through grounding. Feel into your body and notice all sensations from head to toe ... this will bring you back in. Ground your roots deep into the earth. Physically stand or sit on the earth (barefoot when possible). Eating food, drinking water, or using essential oils from trees such as cedar, cypress, or pine will also help ground you.

#2 Becoming Invisible: Like the story I shared, if you have ever felt like you were invisible with other people, chances are you pulled your energy field in so close, you became energetically invisible. This often occurs when something in our environment feels threatening to us, even if on an unconscious level. Instinctively, we shrink our energy field so small we are barely detected by the people around us. Even though they can "see" us, our energy doesn't register and we become invisible to their consciousness.

The Shift: First, ground yourself pulling energy up from the earth to strengthen your field. Envision your field expanding to about three to five feet around you with a robust white light. Imagine this white light is like a bright light shining out to others. Then focus on your heart center and bring to mind a feeling of love and gratitude. Let this feeling expand within your white light orb. This loving energy and white light are noticeable and protective.

#3 Living Wide Open: When we disperse our energy field beyond the three to five feet range, we can pick up or feel other energy and emotions. Many of us learned to do this instinctively to "read" the other people around us. It served us well then, yet is no longer useful. If we are not grounded (and we rarely are when dispersed), the energy from others can be unsettling and may adhere to us.

The Shift: As with leaving your body, the remedy is to ground and pull your energy in. We can use the ability to disperse "on command" when we want to gain information (such as in animal communication). Doing this consciously while grounded will give us information about our surroundings or specific beings without being susceptible to others' negative energy.

29

Energy Interactions

AS CHILDREN, WE WERE OFTEN ON HIGH ALERT as we sent our energy out to others, causing us to expand our energy sensing abilities. This ability has given us gifts and also made us more sensitive. Expansion makes us more aware on an energetic level of everything going on around us and in the entire world. However, when we sense energy on this level, it can feel like a constant barrage of stimulus which in turn often creates anxiety, depression, and alarm. Once we learn how to disengage from this outside energy and strengthen our energy field, we can find more peace in our everyday lives. We can then find the energy to step into our mission and passion.

Energy Exchange happens constantly. People

who "steal" or "drain" energy from others don't consciously know they are doing this. Whenever we are with others, we share energy and an exchange takes place. In healthy individuals, it is a sharing of equal give and take. For example, you have coffee with a friend and they whine for a little while and you listen compassionately and then you whine for a little while. This is a healthy exchange. It wouldn't even need to be whining. You could be sharing something exciting happening in your life and it's still taking energy. You want their attention, which takes energy. It becomes toxic with the person who goes on and on and never lets you get a word in. You feel drained after the conversation because all they did was take.

Those who have not learned how to work with their energy body "steal" energy because it's all they know. It's not conscious action, but a survival tool working from a deeper level. We need to have compassion for ourselves and for others because energy management is not openly taught in our society.

Abuse steals energy. As children, we didn't know all the reasons the abuse felt bad to us, but one of the reasons is that when people abuse other people (or criticize, take power away, humiliate, tease, etc.) they are actually taking energy. We came to expect people to "take" or "drain" our energy without understanding what was occurring. It made us feel bad then and still does today. We didn't understand what was happening, but now we do, and now we can protect ourselves. It is important to note here, that the energy they "took" is easily replaced. They may have drained us on many occasions, but we always have more energy available to us from an infinite source. Nothing is missing from you.

We learned to take energy too.

Yes, because we were exposed to those who take energy, we too learned to take energy. Everyone takes energy. We can be mindful how we are using our energy now and how to replenish our energy without taking from others. Maya Angelou is famous for her quote, "When you know better, you do better."

30

Energy Boundaries & Attachments

As DESCRIBED EARLIER, we each have a personal aura or energy field that goes approximately three to five feet in a complete orb around us. This means it is about three to five feet above our head and below our feet as well as around our body. This is considered our energy "boundary." When others come close to us or touch us, their energy field overlaps with ours. In a sense, they have penetrated our boundary...and we theirs. This in itself is not a problem. It becomes problematic when we or the person walks away and our energies are still intertwined. This means an energetic attachment has occurred. This is often referred to as an energy cord.

When we come into the world, we have an energetic attachment to our mothers and fathers. It is especially strong with our mothers. In a perfect world, this attachment provides us with a sense of security and safety in the world. Then in a healthy relationship, this attachment diminishes as we develop our own healthy self-identity. We will always have an attachment with our parents. Before eight or nine years old, the energy cord is like a heavy seaman's rope. Ideally, it then becomes more like a strand of fiber optic cable, allowing light to flow to connect us, but not a cord which feeds off of each other. Carl Jung refers to this as individuation.

If you did not have a healthy exchange with your parents when you were young due to abuse, neglect, or abandonment from the parent, or a parent with mental illness or addictions, you could have been left feeling unsafe in the world. If you had an overprotective parent, you may find yourself still strongly attached energetically with your mother or father. This is not permanent damage, but requires self-parenting and energy healing to restore the vibrancy of your aura.

We create energy attachments with our siblings, other family members, friends, partners and co-workers. If the attachments are strands of fiber optic cable that provide us connection and intimacy, then all is well. If they are large cords that drain us, then we need to correct them. Addressing these energy cords is the next step beyond Grounding and the Energy Mastery meditation.

Signs You Have Unhealthy Attachments
- You obsess about someone or a situation.
- You replay old conversations with them in your head.
- You feel drained after talking to someone.
- You dread being around this person.
- You walk away from a conversation feeling inadequate or less than.
- You always end up in an argument.

What Creates Unhealthy Attachments

Our emotions create our energy bonds with other people. In order to release the energetic aspects, we must also address the emotion that created it. We can address our emotion and release the cord, but we cannot affect what they do. We don't have control over their feelings. Fortunately, we don't have to change them to alter the attachment.

Here are some of the primary situations that create unhealthy energy attachments. You may see yourself or others in these roles.

The Rescuer: Wanting to be the hero, to save someone, to rescue them, or to heal them are all ways of taking energy from another under the guise of "helping." Supporting someone can be done without taking energy. The difference is that healthy support is provided in a way that empowers others to care for themselves, not to be dependent upon the helper.

Drama Queens & Kings: Becoming involved in another's emotional drama or story will energetically suck you in. This is also true if you are sharing your own drama or story with another. Some people live for drama. They feed off of others by sharing their drama and getting attention.

Filling the Esteem Void: People who feel inadequate or as if they are not enough look to others to fill the void within them. These people will feel needy. They look to others to gain approval and validation in order to feel whole. Unfortunately, this void can only be filled by approval and love from self. When they try to get this from another, it can be energetically draining.

Sexual Relationships: A sexual relationship with another also establishes an energy exchange. It is very important this be mutual. If one person desires another sexually and the feeling is not returned, the "not interested" party will feel the other's energy. Disconnecting from this energy will release the discomfort.

No Place for Blame

The hardest part of understanding energy attachments to others is the realization that some part of us has permitted this attachment. It may be an unconscious belief we hold but there must be agreement on our part. Getting quiet and honest about what you are receiving from the attachment is where you must begin in order to change the nature of your attachment. Once you recognize your part and are ready to release your end of it, the rest of the process will be easy.

An Example

In a healthy attachment between a student and teacher, the student is guided by the teacher; the teacher respects the student's ability to grasp the topic, and acknowledges he/she also learns from the student.

In an unhealthy attachment between a student and teacher, the teacher needs the student to validate self-worth. He/she tend to be condescending to the student. This often happens because the student holds a belief they are inadequate. Because the teacher reinforces this belief, the student is also buying into the attachment.

To shift this relationship, two things could happen: the teacher realizes he/she is using the student to validate self-worth and make changes within to accept herself as she is. Or, the student could realize his worth, stand up to the teacher's condescending attitude, and sever the relationship.

Another more enlightened outcome would look like this. The student realizes she is not inadequate, and on some level, they agreed to this situation. Because she wants to change this dynamic but also value what the teacher has to teach, the student can first own her power and claim her energetic space. Next, she would visualize the energy cord with the teacher dissolving into a healthy fiber optic cord. It's also necessary for the student to believe the teacher is capable of being fair, that is, capable of engaging in a mutually beneficial energy exchange.

Shifting Attachments

If you feel you have unhealthy energetic attachments or "cords" with another person, use the following steps to reclaim your energy and create a healthy attachment.

Get Quiet: Let go of other distractions and take a few moments to practice heart coherence or heart centered meditation.

See the Attachment: Close your eyes and in your mind's eye see where this attachment is on your body. Is this person attached to a specific chakra? What does the cord look like? How does it feel to you?

Find the Benefit: Ask yourself, "What am I gaining from this attachment?", or "What belief do I hold that is keeping me attached in this situation?" Emotions such as anger and resentment can keep us bound to the other. If we are attached to being right and hanging onto these feelings because we feel entitled, we can keep ourselves attached. This introspection requires honesty and gentleness. Often the beliefs we hold onto served us at some point. This may also require being a loving parent to your younger self.

Visualize: When you feel confident you have shifted your belief or let go of your need for the attachment, you are ready to change the cord. Visualize the cord shrinking down to a very small fiber optic strand that just touches the outside of your energy field. This strand does not take energy from you; it only keeps you lightly connected to this other person. Now, see the place on your body where the cord was attached. Fill this area with a beautiful healing white light or the color of the corresponding chakra. See your entire aura filled with light. You can also bring in a specific type of energy to fill the void. If the attachment left you feeling unloved, you can bring in loving mother energy. You could call on a spirit animal or archetype with characteristics that will support you. For example, you could call on an elephant if you needed to fill your void with strength and power or bear if you need to feel motherly love.

Final Detachment: Let go of any ill feelings towards the other person and acknowledge it was a mutual agreement no longer serving either one of you. If appropriate, allow yourself to forgive the other person or yourself. Let go with love.

Important Note: With some attachments, you might not want even a light strand connecting the two of you. In this case, dissolve the cord completely and see the other's energy go back to them while all of your energy stays with you. Proceed with filling any void in your aura by visualizing a healthy vibrant and complete aura.

About Cord Cutting: Many energy advisors recommend "cutting cords" by visualizing using a knife, chainsaw or other device. This form of cutting creates a sense of violence I believe can be felt by the other person, if only subconsciously. My philosophy is to gently dissolve a cord completely when needed. I choose this visualization, realizing all people come into our lives for a reason. I believe we have Soul agreements and those who irritate and wound us the most likely agreed to play the villain for an experience we chose to have in this incarnation. People who behave with disregard for others, with anger, hatred, or prejudice, do so from their wounds. It is their pain speaking to you. Understanding another's pain as a source of their behavior engenders compassion. And, because none of us are truly separate, harming another, even when a visualization, only serves to harm us as well.

31

Claiming Your Energetic Space

Our energetic "space," aura, or energy body is our "sacred" space. It is the part of us which is connected to all that is, to Spirit, to the Divine, to the collective consciousness and to our Soul or higher self. When we go through the world disconnected, out of our body, or energetically dispersed, we have essentially abandoned our own sacred space. If we leave our space vacant, it allows other energy to cohabitate with us. Not good. This is why being grounded, present, and in our body is so important.

As with all our energy work, "claiming our space" requires intention and visualization ... and in this case, adding an affirmation and ritual can be very powerful. Here's a ritual you can follow to claim your sacred space. Once you do this, you will feel a shift take place, although you may need to repeat the ritual at some point in the future if you feel you've slipped back into old patterns and vacated your space. Repeat as needed.

Sacred Space Ritual

This ritual works best if you can do this outside, standing on the ground barefoot. If you can't go barefoot, stand outside with leather soled shoes. Stand with your feet about shoulder width apart. Invite all your energy back to you and collect it within your Sacral/Hara chakra, two inches below your navel. Next, move your energy up into your heart and generate a loving feeling throughout your aura. Repeat the following while using your arms length to define your space. (Think of Wonder Woman making a stance to claim her space).

I, (state your full name), claim my energetic space as my own, as my connection to the Divine, as my sacred space. Any energy not belonging solely to me must leave this space now. No other energy may enter this space without my explicit permission. This is my safe and sacred space occupied by my energy, my Soul, my physical body. I am whole, I am loved, I am safe.

Part 3

Restoring Your Emotions, Thoughts & Body

"The best and most beautiful things in the world cannot be seen or even touched. They must be felt with the heart"
—Helen Keller

32

Being Sensitive is Not a Weakness

"WENDY IS SENSITIVE." That's what my second stepfather used to say. He meant I was emotionally sensitive because he had no understanding of what it means to be energetically sensitive. I expressed my feelings and the feelings of everyone else that could not or would not express their feelings. Empaths carry the emotional load for others. In our family, displaying emotions was considered childish. If you were feeling sad or depressed, the antidote was to get off your butt and do something. And sometimes this advice can be useful once you've had an opportunity to fully express how you feel. However, in my family, the opportunity to express feelings was frowned upon and the coping mechanism was to ignore your feelings, stuff them with food, alcohol, or something else. Get over it. Grow up. Being sensitive was seen as a weakness, an attitude that pervades our society.

Being sensitive is not a weakness; it is strength. You are not weak or "less than." Your sensitivity is a Super Power. Don't ever let anyone tell you differently.

As Fractured Phoenixes, we experience more emotions than the average person. When emotions are allowed to be felt and released, energy flows freely. When emotions are blocked or suppressed, they block the flow of vital life energy, aka Chi or Prana.

We block emotions by habit or instinctual response. Learned habits come from our early childhood. Children are often shut down when expressing emotions. "Don't cry or I'll give you something to cry about." "Big boys/girls don't cry." "Don't be sad, you'll make Mommy/Daddy sad." "There, there don't cry." And the list goes on. Suppression isn't limited to sadness, grief, or anger. Often children in amazing states of joy are told to "be quiet" or "simmer down."

The bigger message behind our caregiver's inability to allow our tears or laughter is the unspoken message: it's not okay to express what you feel...*your feelings are wrong*. And too easily this is translated by a child as "I am wrong," "there is something wrong with me," "I am defective." Shame and unworthiness set in.

This isn't about blame; I'm sure our caregivers were only repeating what they learned. This is about understanding these unconscious beliefs we hold about expressing our emotions. These erroneous beliefs lead us to repress and block our emotions and thereby, our energy.

Emotions can also be repressed as an instinctual response to a perceived threat. Faced with a tiger, our ancestors would perish if they froze from fear. Instead, those who survived did so by repressing their fear and fleeing or fighting back. Deep within our primitive brain is a desire to repress fear and other emotions, which the brain has determined could harm us if expressed. Repression can be a form of survival.

The problem with repression, aside from keeping us from the whole human experience, is that stuffed emotions are problematic. By not expressing the emotion as it surfaces, we give it power. Stuffed tears become anxiety, anger, or depression. When we suppress the energy of emotion, it becomes stuck in our body. It creates physical, mental and energetic illness.

33

Managing Emotions

MANAGING ENERGY requires managing your emotional life. Emotions are currents of energy expressed through the body conveying information from something you sense outside of you or from within. Emotions are your body's physical and energetic response to the information you take in. As Fractured Phoenixes, we take in significantly more information; therefore, understanding how this works is important for our well being.

Here are three examples of how the energy of emotion can transmit and become stuck or be released.

Person A is driving down the road and sees a cat who has been hit by a vehicle, now lifeless. The information is a cat was killed by a vehicle. The external information comes into the body and the energy and physical feeling is sadness or grief. This may also be coupled with past experience losing a beloved animal. Person A experiences the emotion of sadness and perhaps past grief. As yet, no thoughts are involved. This emotional state is an energetic and physical response to information received. At this point she begins thinking and analyzing: "Stupid driver, why can't people be more careful;" "I miss my kitty so much;" "This world feels so cruel sometimes," etc. The thoughts are not the emotion. The thoughts are *expressing feelings* about emotions. Our emotions are instinctual and physical reactions from our primitive brain to stimuli. Our feelings are our mental reaction to an emotion based on our personal previous experience. Feelings can deepen and anchor the physical reaction to an emotion into the body if the emotion itself is not allowed to be released. Now Person A is immersed in thoughts about the emotion but not releasing it. She is anchoring the physical reaction more deeply in the body and anchoring those thoughts in the brain. She continues to think about how sad she is, how this is upsetting, but she doesn't feel into her body. It is likely she is not in her body energetically at this point as a learned reaction to sensing the emotion.

Person B responds differently. The one who unconsciously avoids her feelings, someone who typically dissociates, will see the cat and quickly shift the mind to something different. "I need to get the car washed." The information and energy which came to her was the same, but she shut it down immediately. The emotion and physical response is still repressed within her body. Over time, this leads to physical illness and often medicating with alcohol, food, work, or other "releases."

In both cases, the emotion is repressed. In Person A, it was acknowledged and intensified but not released. In Person B, it wasn't acknowledged or released. One person is consciously sad, the other unconsciously. The energy of the emotion is stuck in the body. Imagine water flowing through a pipe, and then someone puts a cork in the middle of the pipe. The water cannot move through. More water comes in and meets the water blocked by the cork. Eventually, the pipe breaks (think explosive melt down) or the system shuts down and no more water can come through. This is how repressed emotions act in our body and energy system.

Let's look at one more possibility.

Person C drives down the same road and sees the cat's body. She knows from experience this is hard for her to see. She takes a deep breath and feels into her body. She's aware of the sadness and her anger at the driver. She notices tightness in her belly. She breathes more deeply into her belly, allowing the energy and tightness to expand. She's not trying to expel anything; instead she's giving the emotion room to expand.

She's feeling emotion as a physical sensation. She isn't fighting sadness with her thoughts. She understands her emotion and feelings are a natural response to her experience. She knows dwelling on what happened won't fix anything and will lower her energetic vibration and trap the emotion. She continues to allow the physical sensation of sadness to expand until it dissipates. She understands the emotion and physical sensation will dissipate, as she has practiced this many times. She now consciously chooses to think about something that brings her joy and shifts her energy.

In his book, *The One Thing Holding You Back*, Raphael Cushnir likens emotions to weather, constantly passing through your body. To experience the slight changes in the weather, you need to be attuned to your body and physical sensations. Just as we learn to manage our energy by becoming present and familiar with how our energy feels, we can learn to manage our emotions by tuning into our body and feeling the physical sensations of emotions. The Checking In process is very useful in this regard.

Here's a quick four-step process to help you process emotions and avoid energetic blocks in your body.

Four Steps to Allow Emotions to Flow

Step 1) Awareness: It begins with awareness. When we are in the present moment and energetically "in" our body, we can notice emotions as we experience them. Practice the techniques for being present in your body several times a day.

Step 2) Consciously allow releasing: When you sense an emotion, scan to find the physical sensations in your body. Pay close attention to how it feels. Notice all the nuances of the physical sensations. Breathe into the sensations and allow them to expand. Our natural tendency is to tighten down around the sensations to block them. We want to do the opposite. Notice. Allow. Stay with the sensations and eventually you will feel the sensation dissipate.

Step 3) Detach: As you feel into these sensations, let go of any stories around them. Work at not judging. Emotions are just information. Not good or bad. This isn't about WHY you feel this way. The more we try to dig into the past to figure out why we have feelings, the more we attach to those feelings. It's a fine line between an understanding of a hurt or experience from the past versus picking the feeling apart and wondering why you still feel that way, why they did what they did, etc. Staying in the past isn't helpful. Let it go by being consciously in the present.

Step 4) Keep the pipe flowing freely: As you go forward, become aware of emotions as they arise and allow them expression so they can be released allowing your energy to flow. Use the process shown with the example of "Person C."

Emotions & Trauma Cause Physical Pain

As I BEGAN TO PROCESS THE MEMORIES from my child-hood, the body and energy work I received was as important as my cognitive therapy. I experienced what body workers understand: emotions, especially from traumas, can remain in certain areas of the body and during massage or energy work, the emotions can release. My "fibromyalgia" was relieved as I allowed the buried memories to release from my body as well as my mind. Trapped emotions can cause significant physical pain because the body is tightening to hold the emotion in. It's an unconscious reaction our body learned to resist experiencing emotions.

Years ago I experienced excruciating pain in my neck and shoulder area that had developed over a couple of days. I don't remember what helped me link the two but then I realized I was filled with anxiety about something happening in my life, anxiety I had been trying to shut out. I took the time to feel into the anxiety, to breathe into it, and within about ten minutes the pain was completely gone. As I worked with the physical release, I let go of the story I was telling myself, creating the anxiety. In the present moment there was nothing to create anxiety; it was my concern for a future event and the story I made up causing the anxiety. I'm not suggesting all pain is the result of trapped emotion, but it's worth exploring if you experience pain.

Trauma trapped in our body can cause significant pain and illness. Our bodies are designed to release fear and trauma immediately after they occur, but we're often blocked by circumstances or a belief that such releases are not okay. If we were to go on a long run after a scary event, we would release the trapped fear. Unfortunately, our modern lifestyle rarely includes running when we are stressed. Animals show us this stress-releasing process all the time. Dogs will "shake" vigorously after experiencing a stressful event. The next time you take your dog to the vet notice how they shake as soon as they are done and off the table. It's how they disperse the stress.

Our body plays another role in the pain/anxiety feedback loop. Study of the vagus nerve has helped us understand that our body sends messages more often to our mind, than our mind to our body. When we say we have a "gut feeling," it's true because our stomach sends a significant amount of information to our brain.

Tight muscles signal neurochemical reactions, which create feelings of anxiety, whether the tightness is because of a physical cause, tension, or inactivity. It makes sense when you think about our evolution. Tensing muscles is how the body prepares for flight, but if the body never moves from tension to activity, a sense of fear and anxiety set in. As Fractured Phoenixes, we may habitually tighten our muscles as a response to stress. If we experienced abuse, it's a natural reaction to tense the muscles in anticipation of a strike or kick. You likely still respond to stress this way. To counteract habitual muscle tension, engage in physical activity, stretching, and especially yoga to allow the tension to release and quiet the mind. Also effective is guided meditation, where you consciously relax all the major muscle groups in your body.

Resources for Releasing the Old

ALL OF US HAVE TRAPPED EMOTIONS and unconscious beliefs that keep us from living to our fullest. As Fractured Phoenixes, our early life experiences caused us to suppress emotions and believe falsehoods about ourselves. Even though you may have done the difficult work and examined your beliefs and feelings, on a conscious level, there is still another layer.

There is a saying I find true. "In order to heal it, you need to feel it." This doesn't mean you have to go back and rehash traumas, but you need to acknowledge the trapped emotion by feeling it. This process is much simpler than you might imagine, and delivers remarkable benefits.

If you've been detached from your body, take time

to get quiet, bring your energy fully into your body (visualize all your energy coming back to you and filling your body), and notice what you feel. Scan your body noticing (not judging) all sensations. It helps to start at one end and work to the other, such as from your feet to your head. Then use the *4 Steps to Allow Emotions to Flow* process (Chapter 33). However, as I've mentioned before, if "feeling" your emotions becomes overwhelming, leads to hyperventilating, tense muscles, intrusive images or thoughts, leaving your body or other similar sensations, stop and seek professional help.

Following are other techniques which I have found useful.

Advanced Integrative Therapy (AIT): developed by Dr. Asha Clinton is "a powerful yet gentle treatment that heals body, psyche, and spirit." It heals the energy field around traumatic experiences and addresses negative beliefs by instilling more functional, positive beliefs. I have been trained to help others with AIT.

Somatic Experiencing ©, is a process developed by Dr. Peter Levine, one of the most influential researchers and authors in understanding the effects of trauma on humans. Early in his career, Dr. Levine made the connection between how an animal processes trauma via the flight or fight system, and how we as humans typically short circuit this process. Studying animals and his psychotherapy patients, he eventually developed the Somatic Experiencing © process. The process requires working with a trained practitioner. You can locate one near you by going to the website. www. healingtrauma.org.

EFT: Emotional Freedom Technique or Tapping: This technique is based on the energy meridian system. It involves light tapping with your fingers on end points of meridians on your body. It was originally developed by Gary Craig but has been adapted by many others. There is a great deal of free information about this on the internet. Dr. Mercola's website has a demonstration. For free webinars on EFT, go to www. thetappingsolution.com. EFT or Tapping has been used successfully to reduce anxiety, and overcome fears, depression, physical pain, and illness.

The Emotion Code, **by Dr. Bradley Nelson:** This book helps you understand the inner workings of the subconscious mind. Bradley provides a simple technique to help you release trapped emotionally charged events from your past. These "trapped emotions" are in an energetic form. They can create pain, dysfunction and even disease. They can also affect the choices you make and how you think about events in your life. His technique uses some of the same principles as Emotional Freedom Technique or Tapping. You will need to find what feels best for you.

36

Self Acceptance

THE MORE COACHING I DO, the more I realize all struggle, regardless of what area of your life it is in, (abundance, relationships, anxiety, sensitivity, living your mission) at its most basic form comes from not accepting yourself as you are right now. This means not accepting how you see yourself and not accepting how you feel.

If we can find a way to be more accepting of ourselves and how we feel, everything else will fall into place. I have found this to be true in my life. The more accepting I am of what I look like, what I do and how I feel, the more ease and joy I have. That doesn't mean I have this all figured out. None of us do. It's an ongoing process we get to practice every day. If we can allow small improvements and not expect perfection, we will build acceptance over time. It's not about perfection, but consistency in noticing where we are at, and accepting what we are feeling, or redirecting critical thoughts to something more compassionate.

If you believe you have to change yourself because you feel you are not okay as you are, or be different somehow to be at peace and have what you want in your life, you won't succeed. We can't change by rejecting parts of us. We have to find a way to accept all of who we are, even the fat and ugly parts. As we lose the "should," we move forward. You know, I should be further in my career, I should be fit, I should be more fun to be around, blah blah blah. That shit doesn't work. And the tricky part is, the more you move towards what you want in life, the more your feelings of unworthiness come up. This is because the part of you that doesn't feel worthy, *and we all* have this part, the unworthiness in your subconscious is whispering "Who do you think you are to have this?" Fortunately, the more your unworthiness comes to the surface, the more healing can take place. You may have heard the saying "What you resist, persists." And it's true. The more you try to push away the aspects of yourself you don't like, the more they will surface.

So the simple solution is to stop rejecting yourself. I'm going to tell you a story I think might help you with this.

I was in a circle of women. These were conscious,

loving women who in general have a great deal of self-awareness. They have all done substantial personal work. We were talking one day about our breasts. What shocked me was how every woman in the group was unhappy with her breasts or her body in some way. In my view, most of these women had amazing bodies. I couldn't imagine them not being thrilled with how their bodies were but every one of us had negative experiences, (many going back to childhood), that caused us to reject how we looked. So I want you to hear this. You are not alone. We all have feelings of being "less than."

The second reason I tell you this story is to emphasize that, as each of us shared our perceptions of our bodies in this group of loving women, a profound healing occurred. Knowing that others also feel insecure is helpful. Being vulnerable with people who are safe and can hold space for your vulnerability heals your wounds of unworthiness. Being witnessed, heard, and seen is crucial to self acceptance. This isn't a loner job. That's the beauty of having a group of supportive friends. We can allow ourselves to be vulnerable in a safe container, and through our sharing, healing occurs. Of course, one thing to keep in mind is when someone is holding the space for another, there is no fixing, no coaching, and no teaching. An open heart and active listening is all that's required.

Christian Pankhurst of Heart IQ has been hosting

experiential groups for about ten years. His work centers on the healing that takes place in what he calls an *amplified field.* This is a group of individuals who lovingly and without judgment hold space for people to feel their emotions and share vulnerabilities. It's very powerful stuff. But you don't need an entire group. This can happen with one person. He explains that because our wounds were created from us feeling disconnected from the important people in our life, we need others to witness our wounds in order to heal them. It doesn't mean we can't do work on our own to improve self care and self talk. But it is our relationships, intimate, family, friends, and coworkers who will show us what needs to be healed. His first book is a good read, *Insights to Intimacy.* Heart IQ is some of the most heart connecting work being done on the planet.

Most of what we reject in ourselves comes from past experience which left us feeling disconnected from the important people in our lives. Because these others were part of the disconnection and wounding, we need people to help us heal. Other people are mirrors, reflecting back to us the parts of ourselves we reject or don't accept. I've been aware of this for decades. And I don't always like that I'm aware, because I know if something about someone really gets under my skin, it's because I know it's something I reject in myself. I have a difficult time expressing anger because it wasn't safe to be angry as a child, so I tend to judge people who are angry. And as much as I try not to judge others, I always will. Everyone judges others to some extent.

Anger is one of those emotions we've deemed as negative and it isn't, really. Calling any emotion negative is a judgment we've made. There really isn't such a thing as a negative emotion. It's just energy. When we can be with the emotion without judgment, it will easily pass through. More likely though, we repress the emotion we don't want to feel. Then anger becomes rage, sadness becomes depression, fear becomes anxiety or panic. Even love repressed can become needy and possessive. It's not the anger or sadness that causes us pain; it's our resistance to the anger or sadness. When we accept whatever emotion that surfaces, and allow ourselves to experience it, without any stories about it, it just passes through. This acceptance of all emotions is part of our healing. If we begin asking why do I always feel this…, or going into a story about the anger or sadness or whatever, we end up giving it much more power and it takes a hold of us and brings us out of the present moment, either into the past or future, and keeps us from being happy.

The goal isn't to be happy all the time either. There is something known as the "spiritual bypass," where people say they have ascended or released all the energy of negative emotions and now only experience love and joy. I say BS. First, as I said there really is no such thing as a negative emotion. Second, life happens; feelings come up. We're human. Sadness and grief will happen. Anger and fear will happen. It's okay. We notice, we feel, and we allow them to pass through.

In addition to accepting our range of emotions, we also need to become aware of our inner critic. The ranting voice which, while trying to keep us safe, is actually keeping us stuck.

As children, we internalize what we observe and hear from others. We're absorbing ideas and words before we have the capacity to discriminate truth from fiction (or other people's crap). We are also completely dependent upon the adults who care for us. We have a survival instinct to please the caregivers so we can be housed and fed. In our innocent minds it's easy for us to internalize criticisms and/or teasing or protective instructions we hear, and take them to heart. Our child mind develops this inner voice to be vigilant to our behavior so we can please those around us, and in return, be cared for. This isn't to blame parents, teachers, clergy, etc. Though some might justifiably be to blame, it won't help us at this point. Most of them are merely repeating what they were told as children and what they still hear from their inner critic.

Unfortunately, we can learn early in life how we don't measure up, that we need to do something special or be different than we are in order to be okay. We believe our survival depends on "doing right" or pleasing, and our inner critic is born.

Quieting the Inner Critic

- First, become conscious of the attacks you are making on yourself so you can change the dialog and become more gentle and compassionate. If you don't notice them, you can't re-frame them. A meditation practice can increase your awareness.

- If you're feeling anxiety, stop and recall your recent thoughts. Have you been criticizing yourself? Do you sense shame or guilt?

- Re-frame the thoughts in your head. Picture yourself at three or four years old. Imagine this child saying these things to herself. What would you say to her? Tell her the comforting words she needs to hear.

- Eliminate the word "should" from your vocabulary. Replace it with "get to" where possible. "I should go for a walk" becomes "I get to go for a walk."

- Embrace the word "yet." I haven't gotten the job I want...YET. Your words are powerful. Speak what you desire and intend, not what you don't have.

- Ask yourself: If my best friend said this out loud to herself, what would I say to her? *Be your own best friend.*

- Keep in mind your inner critic is trying to protect you; she's just not effective. Help her by enlisting her help. You can dialog with this voice and let her know what she is saying isn't true or helpful. Do this gently, as if you are conversing with a young child. Then ask her to support you by reminding you of what you do right. This may seem a bit bizarre but it works.

Self compassion and self acceptance help you to be motivated, passionate and to take responsibility. It's not self-indulgent, and it's not selfish. It leads to better relationships and to more joy.

When it's safe to make a mistake you are not only gentler with yourself, you are more compassionate with others. The more you accept yourself, the more love you bring to the world.

Self Care & Resources for the Fractured Phoenix

BEFORE YOU CAN BEGIN TO FULLY ENGAGE the gifts of your experience, you need to become a warrior for your own healing and self care. It's easy to neglect ourselves when we experienced neglect as children. Now, we can take our power back and nurture ourselves.

Through my sensitivity and that of my clients, I've learned some key areas to keep the energy body and emotions healthy. Here, I share these insights with you, my fellow Fractured Phoenix.

Practicing Self-Care

Develop Awareness: Knowing what you think, feel and want is the first step. We often are so used to listening to old programming and following what others tell us we should think, feel or do, we have no idea what we actually think and feel.

Recognize your needs: When we don't practice self care, we often ignore our own needs. Begin by becoming aware of your needs. Often we put others before ourselves. Identify your needs and make them a priority. It's about doing what feels right for you.

Exercise the word No: This tends to go along with recognizing your needs. If you consider how a request feels in your body as you think about it and it doesn't feel good, just say no. You have to set healthy limits so you don't deplete yourself. It's like being on the airplane when they tell you put your oxygen mask on first, because you can't help anyone if you can't breathe. This doesn't mean you're being selfish, because when you ignore your limits, you often end up feeling resentful.

Practice good self-care: As you begin to treat yourself more gently you will find it easier to nourish yourself in other ways such as healthy eating, exercise, lots of rest and being social.

Forgive yourself: Put the stick down. All of life is an experiment and the only way you will never fail is if you don't try. Failure is just learning how not to do something.

Other Tips for Self Care

Energy Work: An energy practitioner can help keep your energy flowing freely. As a Fractured Phoenix, this is as important as good nutrition and exercise. There are many different types of energy work including Reiki, craniosacral therapy, sound therapy, crystal therapy, chakra balancing, reflexology, and more. Find out which forms and practitioners resonate best with you. If you don't know any, ask friends or find companies in your area that sell natural products, offer massage, acupuncture, or chiropractic. These places tend to offer or know of local energy practitioners to recommend. A once-a-month treatment until you become more skilled at managing your energy is helpful.

Pacing: Scheduling down time or alone time after being exposed to stimulating environments is one more way to practice self care. Pacing yourself on a regular basis will keep you physically and energetically healthy. When you are tired, sick, or overwhelmed, you are more susceptible to taking on others' lower vibrations. It is okay to say no when you need to. For example, if I am traveling for business or pleasure, I always give myself two to four days (depending on the length and intensity of the trip) to regroup before resuming my regular work schedule.

Be Open To Receive: Energy works within a natural balance of giving and receiving. When we only give or only receive the natural cycle is disrupted. This is true for all energy including money, time, and love. An exchange of equal proportion is important. If you give all the time and do not receive, you are not engaging this mechanism. It is just as important to receive as it is to give. We are often taught as children to not be selfish, to give without receiving. It is okay and it is necessary to receive.

Look at Who is Around You: Surround yourself with positive people who share your ideals, who support your true self and spiritual growth. Since we are energetic beings and are affected by others energy, it is important to avoid those who drain us. When circumstances do not allow us to avoid an energy drainer, we can protect ourselves by grounding our energy or allowing the other's energy to pass through.

Turn off the Violence: Turn off the TV news, the radio news, social media and any shows with violence. There is nothing in the news you need. If something happens you need to know, someone will tell you. The news is distorted to negative perspectives because drama sells. Keep it out of your life.

Use Music or Sound: Music and sound are very powerful means of altering/raising your vibrations. There are CDs available for this purpose. One I recommend is The Divine Name by Gregg Braden. Or use your favorite music, depending on the mood you want to generate. There are also tools such as singing bowls, crystal singing bowls, and chimes. All of these introduce a higher vibration that your energy body will attune to. Singing, chanting, drumming, and movement can also be very powerful for shifting vibrations.

Energy Movement and Visualization Techniques:
Here are some techniques and ideas for moving, restoring, clearing, and protecting your energy field. Try them out and see what resonates with you.

- Energy Fluffing: (From Donna Eden) You can strengthen your energy field by simply fluffing your energy, moving your hands one over the other from toes to head and down the sides while taking in deep breaths.
- Zip Up: (From Donna Eden) To shield yourself from others' energy, or to prevent yourself from leaking your energy to others, here is a simple exercise. Starting at your pubic bone, reach down and zip up to your chin as if you are closing a zipper. Do this three times.
- Plexiglas Tube: Envision that you are contained in a Plexiglas tube that allows you to see everyone and everything but which contains your energy body with you. This way your energy doesn't inadvertently slip out to others. Keep the tube open at the top and bottom to connect you to Spirit and Earth.
- Energy Tornado: To remove energy not belonging to you, envision a tornado whirling around you, swirling all your energy inside you and casting off anything that doesn't belong to you. Visualize the tornado going counterclockwise for tossing and then you can reverse directions to bring your energy spinning clockwise to ground.

- White Light: Envision that you are surrounded in a bubble of white light that protects your energy body and your physical body.
- The Prayer of Protection: For when you are feeling scared or overwhelmed. "The Light of God surrounds me. The Love of God enfolds me. The Power of God protects me. The Presence of God watches over me. Wherever I am, God is and all is well."
- Practice Heart Coherence: To replenish your energy, practice the heart coherence exercise and after being in gratitude for a few minutes, envision beautiful healing energy coming into you through your crown chakra. You can actually feel your vibration rise.
- Using Water: Water is the ultimate purifier of our bodies and our planet. Use your daily shower or bath as a ritual to wash away all others' energy. Following are two techniques.

Epsom Salt & Baking Soda Baths: Taking a warm luxurious bath with added Epsom salts & baking soda provides detoxification for your physical body and energetic body. Epsom salts counteract positive ions (referring to the electrical charge of the ion) that are picked up from Electromagnetic Fields and pulls magnesium into the body, which is calming. Baking soda balances the PH. I use about one cup each per bath.

Coffee & Epsom Salts: This is my favorite for clearing off energies I've accumulated while at family gatherings or in public. Add one cup hot coffee and two cups Epsom salts to your bath water. Immerse yourself in the bath and bring the water from your feet up over your head while holding the intention to release any energy that is not yours. Soak for 15-20 minutes then follow with a quick shower to wash off any remnants.

EMF Protection: EMF or Electromagnetic Field is a broad term which includes electric fields generated by charged particles, magnetic fields generated by charged particles in motion, and radiated fields such as TV, radio, and microwaves. They come from cell phones, cordless phones, appliances, Wi-Fi and the electricity running throughout our homes. Fractured Phoenixes tend to be more sensitive to these frequencies. They can create confusion, anxiety, insomnia, pain, and illness. I use an "Earthing Sheet" on my bed that allows my body to "ground" each night. If you have wireless internet, purchase a modem (Netgear makes one) that allows you to turn the Wi-Fi off and on and only turn it on when necessary. Negative Ion generators can also be helpful. To learn more about EMF's and "Earthing" or "anti-EMF products," I recommend: www.earthing. com for information and products. Standing barefoot on the ground or swimming in a lake, river, or ocean are very grounding and clearing.

You Are What You Eat: This is especially true for a Fractured Phoenix. I don't intend to advise you on nutrition, but I want you to understand the importance of the source of the foods you eat. Because everything is energy, the food you eat is also energy. If food comes from an animal that lived a horrendous life with no regard for it as a living being, avoid this food. The energy of this animal in life: scared, depressed, and ill, remains in the food on your table. You are consuming the energy as well as the nutrients. Those who suffered greatly will carry that energy into the food they provide and into you. If it is not organic, pastured, wild caught or local natural farmer raised, you can assume it did not live a good life. It is better to choose food from animals allowed to roam on pasture or live free in the wild. Animals understand the cycle of life, and are agreeable to being in service this way. Giving thanks and gratitude for their sacrifice will help your body assimilate the nutrients.

Similarly, plant-based foods raised in a natural sustainable manner are a higher vibration and better for your body. When you need to eat less-than-ideal foods, say a blessing for the animal or plant and the energy you receive. This blessing will shift the energy of anything you put in your body.

Flower Essences: Because of their high energetic vibration, flower essences can clear away other energies and lighten your field. Unlike essential oils, which contain concentrated components of a plant, flower essences contain only the energy of the plant. Bach

Flower remedies were long considered the best, and now several other companies make high-vibration remedies such as the Flower Essence Society. In her book The Sensitive Person's Survival Guide, Kyra Mesich, Psy.D, recommends three varieties of yarrow from the Flower Essence Society. White Yarrow (listed just as yarrow), Pink Yarrow, and Golden Yarrow. Yarrow helps balance empathy. White Yarrow strengthens energy boundaries and helps protect you from other's emotions. Pink Yarrow is useful if you find yourself lost in your relationships, if you tend to give too much. Golden Yarrow is helpful if you are more introverted or avoid social situations. If you use alcohol or drugs to numb your sensitivity, Golden Yarrow is good.

Essential Oils: I've used essential oils for energetic, physical, and emotional balancing for over a decade. For overall balancing, geranium, bergamot, and elemi are useful. For grounding, try cedar wood, cypress, spruce, fir, juniper and angelica root. For releasing old trauma, angelica root or yarrow. For addressing grief, loss, or needing to move on: rose, neroli and cypress. For calming: lavender, frankincense, yarrow, or chamomile. To open up and access spiritual guidance: frankincense, palo santo, and angelica root. Use high quality oils and always dilute in a neutral carrier oil such as almond or grape seed oil (one drop in a teaspoon is usually plenty). You can simply inhale the oil or rub on your hands or body. Avoid eyes and mucous areas.

Space Clearing
Cleanse and Clear Your Space.

There are many techniques to energetically cleanse and clear your home, office, car, or any space you visit frequently. It's helpful to do this after others have visited and/or if there have been lower vibration energies such as anger, grief, jealousy, etc. This is also useful if you have recently moved into a new space. Following are techniques I use, and you can also search "energy clearing or space clearing" to find a ritual that resonates with you.

The Process: Regardless of the herb, oil, or element you use, it is vital to always engage with the process in a respectful and sacred manner. Begin with gratitude to the element you are using and an intention for your clearing. For example, "I release all energies and beings in this space with love." Before clearing a space, clear yourself first. Work from front to back, feet to head. When you clear a space, work in a clockwise direction, beginning at the first floor or basement and working your way up. It's a good idea to open windows so any trapped energies can leave with ease. Enter each room, going in a clockwise direction, and smudge or spray into all nooks and crannies. Then move onto the next room.

Smudging: This process uses the smoke of an herb, wood, resin or incense to clear energies from a person or space. While white sage is often used for this purpose, white sage is more appropriately used for creating sacred space. It will clear space, but you might be better off using palo santo for more intense clearing. If you sense an unwanted energy (spirit), use palo santo wood or oil. Palo santo releases negativity and invites in good energies. Sweet grass and copal will bring in good spirits and influences, so often people will follow sage with copal or sweet grass. Cedar is protective. If you feel you need to protect your space or will be doing rituals in a space, cedar is a good choice. You can purchase "smudging kits" at stores and online. If you are using herbs, you will either have a bound stick or loose dried leaves. I have loose leaves in an abalone shell and I move the smoke with a feather. Sometimes I use a smudge "stick" and the feather isn't necessary. It's best to light whatever herb/wood you're using with matches, as they are more natural than a lighter. Some native traditions believe it is important to engage all the elements to clear a space. With the method I described, the abalone shell represents water, the feather represents wind, the herb represents earth and the match represents fire.

Essential oils: If you are bothered by smoke, or are clearing an area where fire is not allowed, essential oils make a great clearing alternative. Mix a few drops of essential oil with water in a small spray bottle. Shake and spray throughout the space using the same process as with smudging. I use palo santo essential oil this way for clearing space. You can also use cedar, pine, lavender, or lemongrass.

Sea Salt: For ongoing clearing, you can purchase a Himalayan Salt Lamp and place in areas you want to keep clear. I have one in my meditation room. You can also use bowls of sea salt in the corners of your home for ongoing clearing. Place the salt in a natural container such as a porcelain or glass bowl. Set the bowls out in the open, in corners of the room. Replace the salt about every two months, more often if the space has lots of traffic or need for more frequent clearing. I use this in addition to the other methods.

The Seven P's of Being a Proactive Fractured Phoenix

Follow these seven steps on a daily basis and you will enjoy more ease and freedom in your everyday life.

Practice Daily Energy Maintenance: It's important to clear and revitalize your energy field on a daily basis. The Energy Mastery Meditation available at www.wendywolfe.com is designed to help. If you take ten minutes each day for this process, you will have more vitality and less energy baggage from others. After a while, you will be able to go through the process outlined in the Energy Mastery meditation quickly on your own in as little as three minutes. Spending more time in meditation can be beneficial too. The more time you spend with your heart open, the more you will be vibrating at a level to manifest your desires and bring more goodness into your life.

Perform Physical Exercise: To move energy out of your body you need to move your body every day. Yoga is an excellent way to move energy. Walking (especially outside and in nature) is also very beneficial. Find a way to move each day by stretching and working up a bit of a sweat with the intention of moving your energy.

Be Present in your Body: Use the Check In technique (the power of grounding and being present) to remind yourself a few times a day to ensure your energy is contained within your body. If necessary, go outside and ground yourself to the earth.

Prepare for Energy Drains: If you know you are going to be in an energy draining situation (even going to the grocery store), prepare by grounding, pulling your energy in, claiming your space and using intention and/or visualization to envision a positive experience.

Process Your Emotions: Notice when you experience emotions and allow them to fully develop and dissipate. You should be able to notice emotions during your Check In process.

Police Your Thoughts: Be mindful of the thoughts you are thinking and as necessary, alter them to a more positive outlook.

Praise the Good: Being grateful for what we have,

no matter the circumstances, will always create more in our life to be grateful for. I recommend keeping a gratitude journal. Each day, morning or night, write down five things you are grateful for.

Part 4

Reclaiming Your Gifts

"If you bring forth what is within you what is within you will save you. If you do not bring forth that which is within you, what you do not bring forth will destroy you."
—Gnostic Gospel of Thomas

Embracing Your Gifts

UP UNTIL NOW, the focus has been on the challenges of the Fractured Phoenix and ways to manage energy, emotions, and thoughts. In the next chapters, we will look at the Gifts of the Fractured Phoenix. The ability to reach out with our energy and sense more acutely than others will prove valuable to gain insights into our life path, connect with animals, guides and if desired, Spirits. We'll begin by looking at Empath Types and Intuitive Gift styles.

There are six different types of Empaths. Some of us experience all of them or a combination. Understanding your more dominant empath type and learning your Intuitive Gift Style will allow you to gain a deeper understanding of how information comes to you.

With this information, you can intentionally develop skills to give you greater insight into your animals, the Spirit world, and Guides who are communicating with you.

For example, if you know you are predominantly an Animal Empath and you are strongly clairsentient, you can use that ability to help animals and their people by sharing where an animal is in pain. You may also want to study energy healing for animals, as you likely will be a very skilled animal energy healer. If you are a physical empath and also very clairvoyant, you may be able to help with people who are ill and "see" the cause of their illness. As with any skill, practice will increase your abilities.

Empath Types

1. **Emotional:** The most common empath type is one who picks up others' emotions. You feel the emotions when you are with someone, watching a movie, or listening to the news. You often have mood swings. People tend to enjoy being with you because they often feel better afterwards.

2. **Physical:** You actually feel others' headaches, nausea, dizziness, etc. You may also be able to channel healing energy to ease physical ailments. You can "see" or "know" another person's illness.

3. **Animal:** You are drawn to animals and them to you. You understand them. You may feel their

emotions, their physical issues, and hear them. You may also receive pictures from them. Animals can understand you as well. They will seek you out.

4. **Nature:** You are very connected to nature. You feel as if the trees and plants are speaking to you. You cry when a tree is cut down. You feel recharged when out in nature. You feel best when you have many plants in your home. When earth events are about to happen such as an earthquake, tsunami, or hurricane you will feel anxious. After the event, you will feel relief.

5. **Matter:** You receive information and even feelings from a photo, objects, or a place. You may receive flashes of visions or feelings from antiques or spaces. You may be able to remote view anywhere on this planet, or anywhere else in the universe.

6. **Spirit:** You feel and/or hear those in other dimensions such as a person who has crossed into Spirit. Spirits come to you and give you information to pass onto the living.

Your Intuitive Gift Style

Just as we each have certain learning styles where we do best, we also have intuitive gift styles that come naturally to us. Our learning styles often reflect our intuitive gift styles. We often have more than one, but typically there is one that is easiest. For example, I learn a physical task best by actually doing it and feeling it in my body. I understand concepts best when I can "see" them, when someone draws me a picture. My strongest intuitive gift is my clairsentience (feeling) followed by my clairvoyance (seeing) although I experience all of the "clairs." See which of the following resonate most with you.

Clairvoyance: "Clear Seeing." This is when we see visions past, present, or future in our mind's eye. Information comes to us in pictures. If you are artistic or visually oriented, you are more likely to receive information in the form of pictures. If you understand better when you are able to see an idea written out or in pictures, you are visually oriented. Remote Viewing is also a form of Clairvoyance. Remote viewing is the ability to connect into a being, a place, or location and see what is happening there. When you connect into another being, you see what they see.

Clairsentience: "Clear Feelings." When we connect with a being, place, or plant and feel joy, sadness or other emotions, or feel physical sensations, this is considered Clairsentience. This is the predominant intuitive style for most empaths. We feel in our body what another feels.

Clairaudience: "Clear Hearing." This is the ability to hear words or sounds in our own mind's voice. This is different than just a "knowing" that comes across. If you learn or retain information best when hearing it, you probably have natural auditory abilities.

Claircognizance: "Clear Knowing." If you have ever had the experience that you just "knew" something without any experience or explanation, you have practiced Claircognizance. Information we would not normally have any way of knowing can come to us through our connection to universal consciousness. This also includes premonitions or forewarning which can be a knowing or in the form of a dream.

Clairalience: "Clear Smelling." If you can smell odors that don't have a physical source, this is Clairalience. Some people pick up on a perfume or tobacco smell from someone who has crossed over into Spirit. This way the Spirit is able to let you know they are around.

Clairgustance: "Clear Tasting." People with a heightened sense of taste (chefs, bakers or foodies) may have the ability to taste something that isn't there. This most often happens with Spirits or when connecting with an animal.

39

Recognizing Signs & Understanding Intuition

You've heard of "women's intuition," gut feeling, sixth sense and listening to your "inner truth." These terms refer to information that comes to us without rational thought. We just seem to "know." This happens when our energy picks up information from the energetic realm where all knowledge resides. As shared previously, as Fractured Phoenixes we often pick up energy and information through our sensitive energy field. Understanding and interpreting this information is crucial.

When information comes to us through our intuition, you might ask "is it my imagination?" And yes it is, but that doesn't mean it isn't true. Your imagination is necessary to receive intuitive messages. It is the doorway. If you shut your mind off completely there is no way for your Soul (or animal or guide) to get messages to you. The ability to imagine and visualize is an asset so let the imagination flow.

Our Souls are often speaking, guiding and providing signs to help us navigate life with more ease. When we recognize and follow the signs, we experience more ease and grace in our lives.

Unfortunately, our childhood education doesn't teach us to hear these messages or notice the signs from our Soul. The language of the Soul is often in metaphors and symbols, so it requires us to not only notice, but to interpret the message.

The Soul might use our dreamtime, animals, songs, people and a variety of other means to get our attention. Learning to notice the signs allows us to feel a greater sense of clarity about our choices. It can also provide a sense of peace knowing there are forces far greater than the small you looking out for your best interest.

To recognize the signs you must first be in the present moment. If your mind is preoccupied with the past or future, it's easy to miss the signs. My Soul often uses animals to bring me messages. When an animal (or bird, insect, etc) shows up in an unlikely place, shows up three times in a row, or finds another way to grab my attention, I recognize this as a sign. To learn the message, I think about what the animal represents to me or refer to "animal medicine" books. These books (or online references) relay the meanings of each creature based on interpretations given by indigenous people since the beginning of time. You can also search on the internet with the animal name followed by "medicine" for a wealth of interpretations.

When searching for meaning in a sign, rely upon what resonates with you. Look for what jumps out and says "yes." Notice how you feel in your body; it will be your guide.

To become aware of how your body responds positively or negatively, try this practice. Get quiet and center yourself. First, think of something you absolutely love. It could be an animal, a person, ice cream, anything that brings you joy. Use all your imagination and senses to experience being with the person/animal, eating the ice cream or whatever your love is. Pay close attention to how your body feels. This is your body in love.

Now, think of something you detest or fear. Conjure up the experience as you did with the love object, paying close attention to how it feels in your body. Where do you feel this fear in your body? What happens to your body? Do you tense? Do you feel nauseous? This is your body in fear/dislike. In the future, when you are considering a choice you will understand the feeling as it arises. Now I suggest you go back to experiencing a loving thought so you can shift out of this energy of fear/dislike.

When you are in touch with your body in the present moment, you can quickly assess how a choice feels to you. This will help you discern messages between ego and Soul. For me, chills, tingles down my spine, tears are all good signs. I know I've hit on the right idea when these sensations arise in my body. If I feel my body contract, tighten, become nauseous, or slump, I know the choice is not right for me.

Sometimes our Soul directs us to a choice that feels scary. Feeling a little anxious because you are stepping out of your comfort zone can be okay. In fact, it's necessary for growth. We can't always stay in the comfort zone. However, if you feel terrified or physically ill, it's not okay. This doesn't mean the choice is wrong forever, but at this time you are not ready. Your Soul will guide you, but will not push you beyond what you are capable of.

40

What is Spiritual Guidance?

SINCE THE BEGINNING OF TIME on Earth, religions and cultures have held the belief that Spirits help those of us in the physical world. From the Oracles of ancient Greece to the Spiritualists of the 1800s, people have been guided by forms of Spirit. The experience of Angels, Spirits of ancestors, guides, and Saints is universal.

My belief and experience is that when we ask for help, we receive guidance. The form the guidance takes is not important. Often times it is a simple "knowing" or a sense of a choice that needs to be made which we refer to as intuition or a "gut feeling." Other times, we may sense, feel, hear or see (in our minds eye) an energy that appears to be other than our self.

These energies can be Spirit Guides, Master Teachers, Animal Spirit Guides, Angels, Archangels, Elementals, and Higher Self. I believe all guidance essentially comes from what we have called God/Source. It is the omnipotence of God/Source that creates and empowers the Spirit Guide, Animal Spirit Guide, Ascended Master, Teacher Guide, etc. A true Spirit Guide is divine and sacred. Its power, wisdom, and actions stem solely from God/Source.

If we allow our ego to take hold, we will look for the Ascended Master or Guardian Angel, or other "highly held" guide to show how special we are. And we are special. *Everyone* is special, none more than another regardless of whom their guide is or how well they are able to communicate with the guide. We are all created of Divine Love, all equally, and this is who we really are.

Angels have shown their presence to me, have protected me, and have found me parking spaces. I have experienced guidance from several sources; Spirit Guides, Animal Spirit Guides, and other entities. The guidance has proved valuable to me but it would not be authentic for me to proclaim I know everything about how this works. I don't believe anyone knows for absolute sure until we go "poof." I share what I have experienced, learned, and how it is has benefited me. Your role is to discern what feels true for you.

One sure test to know if what you hear is true guidance from God/Source is to notice how it feels in your body. Do you feel tingles, love, and acceptance? Do you tear up in a good way? If it does not feel loving, it is more likely the ego. The ego wants to keep us off guard and in fear, which is how it controls us. True guidance from love does not make us feel inadequate, nor does it make us feel judgment towards our self or anyone else. We are all one; therefore, judgment we inflict upon others is truly judgment we have of our self.

I believe our own guides are brought to us in the form we most identify with and can accept. This way the information we need to receive to follow a path of love is easily accepted by us.

How can we discern between "Spirit" based guidance and the ego? "Spirit-based" Guidance comes direct from God/Source and is grounded in love and abundance. It feels loving. "Ego-based" guidance comes from our "small self" the "ego" part of us - and is caught up in fear and survival.

The ego is typically viewed negatively. "She has a big ego" is not seen as a compliment. However, our ego is necessary for our Soul to have an experience in our three-dimensional, dualistic world.

The ego in itself is not bad. Ego looks to protect us from physical and emotional wounding. When we are wounded, our ego has a tendency to protect us in ways more likely to hinder our growth. Our early life experiences taught our ego to be on guard more so than someone without these experiences.

As Spiritual beings having a human experience, the ego, personality, and body serve as our vehicles for our human experience. Our Souls choose the body, the personality, and the experiences that shape our life. The Soul can't come here without a body, so it's up to us to honor and care for our body and ego. The challenge for the Soul is to find a way through the chatter and fear of the ego so it can gently guide us to our grandest experiences.

Spirit-based guidance feels loving, supportive, and gentle while directing you towards gratitude, joy and abundance. It will stretch you to grow and move you forward in your life. It always has your best interest in mind. Spirit knows you are not limited and there is great abundance waiting for you even if it means a temporary inconvenience. Spirit-based guidance empowers you and encourages you to empower others. Spirit wants you to fulfill your mission in life and may give you the same guidance over and over again. You will be encouraged to "leap and the net will appear." As you trust Spirit and follow its guidance, you will be rewarded with abundance in all its forms.

Ego-based guidance is motivated primarily by fear and needs to keep the status quo. Think of FEAR as **F**alse **E**vidence **A**ppearing **R**eal. Ego's job is to keep you safe. It will try to keep you on the safe path. Ego will tell you why you shouldn't do something or can't do it. Ego believes in win or lose, not win-win. Ego will focus on lack in your life and try to convince you that you must take from others to get your fair share. Ego based guidance tends to sound critical and parental.

Working With Spirit Guides and other Helpers

Learning to know and work with your guides and helpers is a journey of exploration and practice. Creating a relationship with these helpers has benefits for our everyday life such as:

- Never feeling alone in the world
- Having support and encouragement
- Feeling protected
- Being creatively inspired
- Gaining guidance for everyday decisions

We each have guides and angels "assigned" to us while we are in physical form. They will protect us (to the extent our Soul has agreed) even if we don't believe or engage with them. When we purposely engage with them, they will be able to provide more assistance. As with intuition, the more you listen and act, the more information will come to you. When we don't engage, there is only so much help they can provide. The key to getting guidance is to ASK.

Some people are afraid they will attract negative or evil spirits if they open themselves to guidance from Spirit. Personally, I don't believe in evil spirits but again, until we go "poof" no one can be certain. You are in control of your interactions and, with simple actions, you can ensure only beneficial spirits interact with you. Whenever I reach out to the Spirit dimension, I use a simple statement to declare my intention. "I invite only those who walk in the light and who honor and support my highest good and the highest good of the planet."

The key to hearing and understanding guidance is to create a relationship with your guide(s). Spending time with and asking questions of your guides will allow you to develop a relationship which will progress and deepen. Scheduling a regular time to communicate and writing down what you learn in a journal will help you increase the awareness and information.

Like your Soul, information from your Guides often comes in dreams, symbols and metaphors. Being in heart coherence allows for interpretation without fear.

It helps to have a place in your mind where you can go when you want to connect with your guides. This is your sanctuary. Start out by discovering this place. Get quiet, ground, and engage in heart coherence. Now allow yourself to imagine a place you would find comforting and beautiful. It might be on a bench by a waterfall, in a meadow, in the woods or in a crystal palace on another planet. It is whatever feels right for you. Once you have this vision clearly in your mind, you're ready to move on. You only need to do this step once. This will continue to be your sanctuary unless at some point you decide you need a new one.

Start out by relaxing your body. Move from head to toe releasing tension. Once completely relaxed, ground your energy and go into heart coherence spending several minutes in the breath work. Allow the energy of love and gratitude to raise your vibration. You can also use the Divine Name CD or other music to help elevate your vibration.

If you wish, invoke a protection around you. For example "I invite only those who walk in the light and who honor and support my highest good and the highest good of the planet."

Now go to your sanctuary and close your "mind's eye." Ask for one of your guides to show themselves and open your mind's eye. "I invite whoever is here to guide me to allow me to see you now" (or something similar). Who do you see?

If you don't see anyone, don't worry. Ask for a name. Ask for a description if you can't see one.

Ask what purpose they serve in your life. What are they here to help you with?

You can also ask them to show you a sign when they are around. Maybe they will touch you; maybe you will feel a tingle. Give them a week to do this.

Ask them "How can I best connect or communicate with you in the future?"

Journal about what you learn. Keep track of your communications.

Ask them for something. Ask for help, insight, a

favor or whatever you need but start out small. As you develop the relationship you can ask for more. Remember you need to ask for them to truly be of service.

This is a partnership. You want to engage their help as if they were a business partner. It is okay to ask for what you need. Don't put them on a pedestal and always be appreciative.

In closing, express gratitude for their presence and help.

Communicating with Animals

MANY OF THOSE who have experienced traumatic childhoods develop close relationships with animals. This was true for me, and over the years, I have found many of my animal communication students also experienced trauma in their childhoods. You may already be hearing messages from animals, yet you might not realize they are actively communicating with you. Here I provide you a process to consciously make connections with animals so you can better understand their needs and desires.

For years I've described my work as "animal communication" and when people ask what that means I often, for the sake of brevity say, "I talk to animals". I even use the clever phrase "Can We Talk?" with a cute photo of my dog Hanna on the cover of a brochure. The truth is, I don't "talk" to animals. None of us do in the way you and I talk to each other.

What I can say is I connect energetically with animals and in doing so, information about how the animal feels physically and emotionally comes to me. Their attitudes towards people, food, medicines, other animals and tasks in their lives come through in feelings, not words. Where they hurt, the level of pain or strong emotions is felt in my own body as I connect. Some part of my being translates the feelings into words or knowing. The words "said" by the animal, are really my translation of the feelings and images I receive when energetically connected to an animal. This form of communication is known as telepathy. Telepathy is defined as "communication from one mind to another by extrasensory means" or a means other than our known five senses. Energy comes to us and is somehow translated into known information.

Here's a good example of the "translating" that happens. Many years ago when I was just starting to communicate, I was confused by conflicting advice on what to do for my horse Smokey's hooves. His early years on the show circuit in Tennessee had created serious hoof problems for him. One day after advice from the farrier, I conveyed to Smokey, "I don't know what you need. Please tell me what you need." Clear as day I heard "Get the fucking shoes off and lower the heels." Now, really, did Smokey know the "f" word? I don't think so. But, the emotion and the intention of what he felt was best for him came through loud and clear. I followed his advice and he has done well for 20+ years. And knowing Smokey as well as I do, he would definitely use the "f" word if he knew it. He would use it often.

Animal Communication is a *two-way* connection and we can transmit information as well as receive it. Frequently, I use images (sent through energy from me to the animal) to help them understand behavior we humans need from them. I receive images back, apparently from the animal. What happens between the animal and me (or others) is not clearly understood by anyone. Rupert Sheldrake has conducted studies which tell us animals are connected to us energetically or telepathically as there is no other explanation for how they know when their owners are returning home. He wrote about it in his book: *Dogs That Know When Their Owners are Coming Home.* My best explanation is we have access to all information in the "collective consciousness" and by tapping into it, we can "know" anything. Even though I may believe I understand how communication works, no one knows for absolute certain (at least until they go poof). The more we stay open to what we don't know and remain curious, the more we allow truth to enter our experience.

There have been many times when my exchange

with an animal feels like a conversation with another human. This makes the "animals don't actually talk" piece challenging. Why this happens sometimes and not always is beyond me and anyone else. I don't feel compelled to know "why". I am content with the understanding that occurs between the animal and me. The results speak the only truth I need.

Through years of teaching others to communicate with animals and my own experience connecting with thousands of animals, I have learned what is important to them and what is necessary to connect with them to receive valid information.

Animals communicate telepathically with their own species and other species when they need to. They take in much more information from their surroundings than we can imagine. This is what has allowed them to survive through the evolutionary process. Typically, they will first rely on body language from their own species or others. But when needed, they will also connect telepathically to derive information about what is going on. They will sense energies and emotions to help them understand what is going on around them. The last method they choose is to listen to verbal communication from a human.

We too are born with the ability to communicate telepathically. As babies, we come into the world relying on the energy dimension more than the physical. We quickly learn others only understand verbal communication (physical) and so we are forced to learn to communicate our needs verbally and in the process diminish our skill of telepathy. Children often communicate with animals, but eventually stop because they are discouraged by adults or they shut down their ability when overwhelmed by stimuli.

Animals are much more sensitive or aware of energy and emotions than humans. It's not that they possess abilities we do not; it's that they continually use these abilities for their survival. Humans have allowed these abilities to atrophy by focusing on verbal communication and external power. Animals are aware of our emotions and energy. When we are stressed, even if we try to hide it, they will know it. Not only do they know it, but they feel it. They have an awareness of all the energy fields around them so when your energy is chaotic they cannot help but feel it. This is how they sometimes "take on" our stuff. Even though they feel our energy, they don't take it on unless it is part of their purpose. We can manage our own energy so it is less intrusive upon them or others.

Our animals pick up on our thoughts and images. Because they are telepathic, our animals often pick up thoughts or images from our minds. This does not mean they completely understand the thoughts or images. They are more in tune with our energy and emotions. Following the communication process I outline shortly, you can be sure they understand what your thoughts or images clearly mean.

Most animals have a strong desire to communicate with their guardians. They already sense your emotions and understand much of what you tell them. They crave a connection with a human when the human is "present." The greatest gift you can give your animal is the calming peaceful sense of being present with them. I invite you to experiment with invoking heart coherence while in the presence of your animals. Each day when I meditate, all my dogs join me in my meditation room and zone out with me.

It is possible to connect with an animal on different levels. Sometimes when we connect with an animal, we are communicating with their physical being, ego, or personality. Other times, it is possible to connect in with the higher self, Soul, or spirit of the animal.

Animals communicate what they are able to. Sometimes an animal knows very clearly what is wrong with them physically and can convey the information to us. Other times they are unaware of the exact ailment and can only share what they are experiencing. Occasionally they have an awareness of what is happening but they choose not to let their person know. Animals do sometimes prefer to hide it from their person if they are dying.

Here are two stories from my communicating experience which demonstrate different ways animals communicated a need to me.

My sister contacted me when she found a lump on

her dog Remmie. She had taken him to the vet, who told her it could be a benign fatty tumor or it could be a cancerous tumor. The only way to know was to do a biopsy or have it removed and then biopsied. He also suggested she could wait and see if it continued to grow. Concerned about her dog, but not wanting to put him through unnecessary surgery, she contacted me. When I connected with Remmie, I was quickly aware that it was a fatty benign tumor, but it was growing quickly and near the spine so should be removed. My sister scheduled an appointment with the vet for four days later to have the growth removed. The night before the surgery, Remmie had difficulty controlling his hind end. The surgery went well, and she called me to report it was a fatty tumor (benign), but was growing quickly, and had already begun to push up against the spine, likely causing the hind end issues.

I would like to tell you that all my communications were this accurate, and while many have been, an actual diagnosis is rare. Animals can show us where there is pain or what feels off, yet I would never rely solely on my information without the expertise of a veterinarian.

Another story illustrates how an animal can communicate what is going on, but may have no clue as to why. A woman contacted me about her horse that seemed a bit off. When I connected in with the horse I could sense his frustration with not being able to use his body as usual. He felt uncoordinated and was physically uncomfortable. While communicating with him, I sensed it was important for him to get a massage and by a specific equine massage therapist I knew. I shared this information with the client and shortly after our session, she contacted the massage therapist. When the massage therapist saw the horse and his movement, she said "I think this horse has EPM" (equine protozoal myeloencephalitis a neurological disease caused by a parasite). She was able to quickly identify the EPM because she had just experienced this with her own horse. A vet was consulted and a positive EPM diagnosis was the result. Because it was caught quickly, the horse made a full recovery. In this case, though the horse didn't understand what was causing his problems, I was guided to the right person to get him the help he needed.

What Can We Expect from our Animal Companions?

Animals are spiritual, energetic beings like us. They chose to come to this lifetime as a specific animal. They are here in a physical body that has been encoded with specific DNA which determines their instinctual nature and is part of the experience they chose. So while we can communicate with them telepathically, we need to support them when living with us forces them to live contrary to their instinctual nature. They can learn to override certain instincts to get along with us two-leggeds, but we also need to learn their language, the language that speaks to their instincts.

Not all companion animals have the same level of instinctual nature. Some are very wired to their animal instincts and struggle living with us humans when we don't allow them to experience them. Most cats do best when allowed outdoors. Horses need to live in a herd outside with available shelter. Dogs need to be able to express their genetic proclivities such as herding, hunting, or searching. Others are content to live with humans and only occasionally have their animal instincts explored.

Behavior can often be addressed using animal communication. Animals are generally willing to make changes to accommodate their guardians. Sometimes they need to be heard; other times they need the person to make a few changes. But...

Animal communication does not replace training. Because they have come here to experience a particular physical body encoded with certain instincts, it is unfair to expect the animals to learn our particular language without seeking first to understand how they communicate. Once we understand how their species communicates, we can then use that information to help them live in the human world through training. Only training that uses positive reinforcement and truly respects the animal should be used.

Following are the guidelines and process I teach in

my animal communication classes. By following these steps, you can connect with animals.

Respecting and Honoring Animals: It is essential that you love, honor, and respect animals for the spiritual beings they are. Even though they are in different bodies, they are no less important or significant than human beings. Conduct your communication to help you understand the animal's point of view. His or her feelings and thoughts need to be heard, felt, and respected. Ego and a need to dominate are not conducive to good communication.

Because animals are under our care, we may sometimes need to negotiate with them and ask them to alter their behavior in order to facilitate health, safety or other concerns. Never use manipulation or deceit. When you ask with respect and appreciation for the animal's point of view, the animals will usually alter their behavior.

Sometimes, instinctual behavior, encoded in their DNA, will prevent them from completely altering their behavior. Honor and praise their willingness to try and remember all of us are instinctual when in a physical body. Also remember your Soul and the Soul of your animal has called you forth to this experience. You are in this relationship to learn about yourself, to learn to love yourself unconditionally, and to love others, two-legged and four-legged unconditionally as well.

Clearing your Energy: First and foremost, communicating with an animal requires that you are centered and clear of any blocking energy such as resentment, anger, jealousy, or guilt. This is not to say it is bad to have these emotions; indeed all emotions are necessary for a full human experience. Rather, it is important to acknowledge these emotions when they are present in a loving, honoring way, hear the information they bring you and then release them so they do not create a block in the flow of your energy.

How you decide to clear your energy or any ritual or practice you choose to develop is completely up to you. It will flow from your own beliefs and practices. I choose meditation, which at times is done indoors and at other times outdoors, both sitting and walking. For me, being completely present to all the feelings in my body and the sounds, smells, and energetic presences around me brings me to a state of openness that facilitates my communication with the animals.

When I have an emotion that needs to be released, I first recognize it, ask it for any message, staying open to the message and not judging myself. Once I feel satisfied that I have explored the emotion fully, I release the energy of the emotion to the Earth. Imagine that the energy is traveling down through your body, through your feet and deep into the Earth to be recharged and reused in whatever way is best for the Earth. You can also imagine a pure white pearlescent light coming into your body through your crown chakra traveling through your body and out your feet clearing, cleansing and healing your entire energetic body.

Opening your heart: This technique is also referred to as Heart Coherence developed by the HeartMath Institute which was discussed earlier. When I first learned this technique I realized it was how I communicate with the animals. Once you have cleared and grounded your energy, focus on your heart area. Then imagine you are breathing in and out through your heart area. Breathe just slightly deeper than usual. Now, focus on your heart breathing and think of someone or something you love or are grateful for. Find this place of love and gratitude. Allow the love and gratitude to consume you.

Connecting with the Animal: Once you feel your heart open and full of love, state your intent (aloud or in silence) to communicate with this specific animal. For example, you might say "I am connecting with Buster, who lives in Chicago with Sally Smith. The communication flows easily to me. I am a clear and perfect channel, the light is my guide." Or you may not say anything; either way is okay. Look at the animal's photo and see them in your mind's eye, as if he/she were right in front of you. Wait quietly. Now you may begin to feel emotions, or physical sensations or you may see pictures or hear words. At this point, you may sense you are connected. Introduce yourself (unless it is your own animal) and ask permission to have a conversation. Ask your questions and then be mindful of your immediate impressions. When you feel an animal's energy, it may feel like warmth in your heart or you may sense fear, anger, or any number of other emotions the animal is experiencing. It is very helpful to write down all your impressions, what you hear, what you feel and what you see. The more quickly you write it down, the more easily additional information will flow to you.

Suspend judgment: Notice if your mind wants to judge or alter the information. Try not to analyze or judge what you are receiving. If you are unclear about an answer, ask another question to verify or clarify. It is okay to let the animal know you aren't sure if you are hearing them or your "monkey mind" (that judging voice in your head).

Starting out: You may find it helpful to begin by practicing with your animals or with a friend's companions. Seek out situations that are non-threatening and allow you to build your confidence as you learn to communicate. Ask for their help and patience and always take them seriously. Writing down what you hear, feel or see is very helpful and highly recommended.

Thoughts and feelings must match words: Remember animals already hear and feel your thoughts, emotions, and energy. Always ask for what you want, not what you don't want. Send pictures of what you want as they don't hear/see the "don't do this" part of the thought. Show the cat a picture of it scratching on the post, using the litter box, etc. Remember, you cannot fake it with an animal. If you are trying to hide feelings from them, it doesn't work. They will be confused when your thoughts/words do not match your emotions.

Believe in your ability: One of the most difficult aspects is to trust what you are hearing is what the animal is communicating. For many who choose to take this path, trust is a lesson they are working on.

Practice, Practice, Practice: We all possess this ability and just like any other skill in life it requires practice on our part to enhance our skill. Just as an athlete needs to practice and keep in shape, so does the animal communicator. We are not looking for perfection as it does not exist in the human experience. We are looking to learn about ourselves, better understand our companion animal's needs and wants and to experience a journey.

Quick Summary of Steps for Animal Communication
- Get quiet, be still, and ground your energy.
- Initiate Heart Coherence:
  - Take a few deep breaths.
  - Focus on your heart center.
  - Breathe as if you are breathing in and out through your heart center.

- Allow a feeling of gratitude and love to permeate your entire being.
- See the animal in front of you in your mind's eye.
- Send a feeling of love to the animal; visualize your heart center connecting with their heart center.
- Introduce yourself or express your wish to communicate.
- Notice what you feel, hear, sense, see, taste, and smell.

As you practice this process, you will eventually be able to think "be quiet and still" and you will move right into the feeling of gratitude and joy and your energy will quickly go to the animal you wish to communicate with.

Part 5

Refueling Your Future with Grace

"It's not your work to make anything happen. It's your work to dream it and let it happen. Law of Attraction will make it happen. In your joy, you create something, and then you maintain your vibrational harmony with it, and the Universe must find a way to bring it about. That's the promise of the Law of Attraction."

—Abraham

(Excerpted from the workshop in Larkspur, CA on Sunday, August 16th, 1998)

How We Create Our Reality

As SHARED EARLIER, the Law of Attraction is a simple energetic law of the universe in which like attracts like. Energetically this translates to energy at one vibration, attracts energy and experiences of a similar vibration. It is a universal law, just as gravity is a physical law of mass.

Because each of us is comprised of electromagnetic energy in both our physical and non-physical (spiritual) being, we create our reality from the electromagnetic energy that is thought, belief, and emotion. The energy of our thoughts, beliefs and emotions attract to us our life circumstances. So if you are not thrilled with your life, examining and changing your thoughts, beliefs, and emotions can and will change your circumstances.

Much of what has been written about attracting what you want in your life doesn't go deep enough to create change. You can recite affirmations until you're blue in the face, but if it isn't consistent with your thoughts, beliefs, and emotions, nothing will change.

Minding Thoughts & Altering Beliefs

Thoughts are a form of energy. When our thoughts frequently conjure up negative scenarios, they eventually become true. Fortunately, the easiest way to change how we create our reality is to change our thoughts. When we observe what's going through our mind, we become aware of our thoughts. This awareness allows us to change our thoughts in an instant; it requires practice and diligence, but is not difficult.

We give *meaning* to everything that happens in our world. The meaning we give is a choice. You can choose to create meanings which bring more peace and joy to your life, or you can choose meanings which create more sadness and anxiety.

For example, say Sue is driving down the road and notices the odometer now has 120,000 miles on it. Her thoughts go to, *Wow, that's a lot of miles. I'm going to need to buy a new car soon. Cars are really expensive now and I don't know how I'm going to afford it. I hate that I can't just go buy a brand new car. Why can't I just win the freakin lottery? I hate not being able to buy whatever I want.* Yada, yada, yada. When you notice yourself on this train of thought, pull the brakes on the engine, because all it is doing is taking you down the wrong track and pretty soon the whole train will derail.

So, what's wrong with this picture? It's true Sue's car has 120,000 miles on it, but does that mean it's going to break down tomorrow? No. Sue is making this part up. We all make up stuff in our heads that isn't necessarily true, but we act as if it is. You can see where the "making stuff up" thought pattern takes her, *I don't have enough.*

The important thing to notice here is Sue is not in the present moment. She is worrying about a problem that doesn't exist in the present moment, and isn't even true. She's giving away her power to create the abundance to purchase a new car by being convinced she can't do it. And she is reinforcing her belief of "I don't have enough."

While affirmations aren't going to save her, the first step she can take is to challenge her thoughts and change them. Is her assessment of the situation really TRUE? No. What could Sue think instead? Well she could stop herself and say "This car has run really well for 120,000 miles. What a great car it is. I'm glad I have such a great car." This is actually true. Now she is reinforcing the idea that *she* drives a great car. By reinforcing this idea, she reinforces her thoughts about what she drives. Someday it may be a different car, but she is changing her thought about what kind of car she drives. This is a much more positive thought.

As she changes her thoughts, she begins to change her beliefs. Our repetitive thoughts become our beliefs. To change our beliefs, we have to change our thoughts. The resulting change in energy will begin to shift life circumstances, but of course there is more.

Our beliefs begin very early in life. Many of our beliefs are unconscious. We aren't aware of how they influence our actions. Additionally, we are part of a collective consciousness which holds a collective belief about "what reality is" which also influences us. Many of these beliefs are so much a part of us we don't realize we hold them. Just as our thoughts influence what we attract to us, our beliefs also attract life circumstances. As Sue continues to believe she doesn't have enough, she continues to attract a reality that confirms she doesn't have enough.

Noticing your thoughts by being the observer and staying in the present (Checking In) is a powerful formula for discovering and altering your beliefs. You may also need to do some Soul searching to uncover other hidden beliefs so they can be brought out into the open and challenged. The easiest way to discover these beliefs is to look at your life circumstances. In Sue's case, she may have some deeply held beliefs about worthiness and may think she isn't worthy of great wealth, or she may have other beliefs about money that keep her from having an abundance of it.

If there are circumstances in your life you are not thrilled with, begin to look for the underlying belief. If money is an issue, what beliefs do you hold about money? What did you learn about money from your parents or others who influenced your values and beliefs? What beliefs have you created from your experiences with money?

This is an example of where you can begin. Once you uncover the beliefs, you can begin to challenge them. Are they true now? When you find evidence to challenge your beliefs, you begin to change them. Add to that monitoring your thoughts and altering them in the moment and you have a powerful combination to begin creating more grace and flow in your life.

This is why it is so important to live in the now. Our power lies in the present moment. Our power of manifestation and transformation cannot lie in our past or we would already have accomplished it. It cannot lie in our future because we create our futures from our perceptions, beliefs and emotions of *this* moment. The more we pay attention and are focused on the now, the easier it is to identify and transform those old beliefs and patterns as well as negative feelings about who we are and any perceived reality that is keeping us off track.

Every moment we are attracting our exterior reality. This is why being in the present moment and acknowledging the moments of joy, laughter, and abundance is important. And remember, you have attracted and created moments of joy and abundance. The great parts of our life are attracted by us too. It isn't luck or someone else's doing; it's all ours.

Try this experiment suggested by Pam Grout in her book *E-Squared.* Pick a thought or belief you have that brings you down. For the next few days, look for evidence of the opposite. For example, if you have been focusing on all the negativity in the world, look for evidence of all the good in the world. Set your mind to work. Ignore and skip by anything that is not good. When you see the good, make a note of it in your mind. Make a BIG DEAL out of it. You will notice as you do this that you see more and more good.

Emotion is the Key to Forward Motion

Our emotions are a forceful influence on the vibration of our energy field. More than anything, feeling genuine emotion of gratitude, joy and love will attract abundance to our lives. The more you can take a moment to truly appreciate when something good happens, no matter how small, the more you pull towards you more of life to appreciate in your future. Noticing sunshine, flowers, a stranger's smile, a wagging tail, or any other small reminder of good and grace will bring you more to be grateful for. Being an optimist who sees the glass half full will always serve you in creating more grace in your future.

This doesn't mean we ignore "negative" emotions of sadness, guilt, or anger. As shared before, repressing those emotions only gives them more power. Noticing them and acknowledging them without judgment allows them to move through your energy body. Allow yourself to feel, cry, and shout or whatever you need to do to express the emotion (without causing harm to yourself or others, of course), then let it go. If you find you have negative emotions excessively, look at your thoughts. Your thoughts and beliefs feed into your emotions. You can reduce the negative emotions by changing and challenging your thoughts.

We are Powerful BUT...

Understanding the law of Attraction allows us to be conscious co-creators. We are powerfully responsible for our lives. People who tend to be pessimists or who are hard on themselves can misconstrue the Law of Attraction and use it to beat themselves up. If a family member or beloved animal companion dies, it isn't because you were thinking negatively! We are powerful, but we do not have power over the choices of another Soul. We may have agreements with those Souls, but we do not have the ability to mess up another's Soul plan.

Please don't use the Law of Attraction to beat yourself up. If you have illness, know the illness is providing you information. There is a reason your Soul chose this. Trust you are exactly where you need to be right now. Everything in your life is unfolding as it needs to. Embrace every bit of good you can find and bask in gratitude.

Seven Steps to Manifesting a Goal or Desire

Here are some specific steps to manifest an intention or desire.

1. *Commit 100%.* You must decide to do it. This might seem obvious, but many times when people put out an intention or desire they muddle it with thoughts like "it would be nice," "I wish I could do this," or " I wonder if this is possible." They might also start asking other people, "Do you think I would be good at this?" "What do you think of this idea?" None of this is commitment. When I left my job at the university to communicate with animals full time, I committed to it. I said, "I am going to be a professional animal communicator full time."

2. *Declare it.* Say it out loud (though not to someone else). You are telling the universe what you are creating. You aren't asking; you are declaring. "I am a full-time professional animal communicator." Make it so.

3. *Seek the Highest Good.* Intend that your intention

or desire manifest in a manner that is in your highest good and the highest good of all. Having it work for everyone leads to more positive outcomes.

4. *Notice Synchronicities.* Once you have declared it, notice over the next couple of days and weeks how synchronicities or resources begin to show up. Know these are coming to you to help you in your manifestation.

5. *Take Action.* When you notice the synchronicities or resources, take action. Small actions in the direction of your goals will solidify your intention. Don't expect something to just fall in your lap (although this is possible). Ask yourself, "what can I do today to move me towards my goal?" Caution: If you're solely focused on taking action, but not committed at the intention level, you create conflict and can sabotage yourself.

6. *Energize your Intention.* Go into heart coherence, and either send your intention out to the universe through your energy, or bring in energy from the universe with your intention. If you are manifesting something you want to bring to the world, (say you want to provide a service, or create a company), that type of intention should be sent out from your energy body to the universe. If you want to draw something to you, like money or a relationship, you would see energy coming from

the universe to you with the intention. Breathe out what you want to "give" and breathe in what you want to "receive."

7. *Let go of Attachment.* Let go of HOW it manifests and what it looks like. Don't allow your small ego self to get in the way of what your higher self has in mind. Often what manifests will be better than you had expected or imagined.

Summary of Manifesting Tips

Be in the present moment. Notice your thoughts, beliefs, and emotions. All of your power lies in the present moment.

Be very careful how you speak. Everything you say after the words "I AM" affects what shows up in your life. We often say, I am sick, I am depressed, I am sad. While it might be true in the moment, you are better off finding a different way to express this if necessary. For example, you could say, "at this moment I am experiencing sadness." It is a temporary experience. It is not who you are.

Change your story. If you tell the same story about yourself, you will get the same results. Make up a new story and tell that as if it is true (and then it will be). Saying "I always get the flu in the winter" is a story. You perpetuate the experience by continuing to tell this story to others. What stories are you telling? How can you rewrite your stories?

Be grateful for all you are and all you have been given. Focus on what you have, not what you do not have. We attract to us what we focus on. If you focus on what is great and beautiful in your life you will attract more of the same. Yes, there are less wonderful things in your life too… don't give them attention and you will not give them power.

To want is to lack. "I want more money" is actually a statement of lack; it implies "not enough." "Money comes to me in ways I can't even imagine" is a more positive spin and focuses on abundance.

Ditch hope, want, and need. These words are not words of commitment or belief. Take them out of your vocabulary if you intend to manifest an intention.

Look for the good in everything. When your thoughts are not positive find a way, even the smallest way, to find a positive aspect of your situation and see it differently. Change your perception of the thought, feeling, or event. Ask/pray to see things differently.

Be gentle with yourself and others. Release blame and shame. Let go of judgment of yourself and others. Love yourself and forgive yourself. Open your heart to others. Forgive, give, and receive.

Raise your vibrations with prayer, meditation, music, sound, massage, Reiki, yoga, Tai Chi, Qigong, or other energy work. You attract to you things and circumstances of a similar vibration. By consciously managing your vibration you will attract higher vibration outcomes.

You deserve good things and goodness in your life.

You do not need to figure out the "how" of bringing something into your life; ask and ye shall receive. Let go of how it will happen; trust God/Source/the universe will provide.

43

Soul Alignment Creates a Life of Grace

Of all the influences on our state of happiness, being in alignment with your Soul or true self is number one. What does it mean to be in alignment?

- When you are in alignment with your true self or Soul, you live life consistent with your deepest values, your mission.
- You understand your mission in life and fulfill it through your actions.
- You are true to yourself and don't succumb to others' wishes for you.
- You don't pretend to be someone you are not.
- You are comfortable in your own skin, wrinkles, fat and all.

- You don't criticize yourself. You are kind and gentle with yourself.
- You act upon nudges from your intuition with trust.

Being in alignment places focus on your own needs, which some might interpret as selfish. It is not. In reality, when we are in alignment, we are immensely more capable of giving to others than when we are not in alignment. Doing for others at the expense of our true self serves no one. Service out of guilt or obligation carries lower vibration energy.

Ask yourself:

- What do I do that serves my true self?
- What do I do that denies my true self?
- How can I add more actions that serve my true self?
- How can I eliminate the actions that deny my true self?

Finding Your Mission

WHEN WE ARE IN ALIGNMENT with our Soul's mission, we find passion and meaning in our life, which translates to joy and gratitude. If you've never given thought to your mission, I invite you try a little exercise to discover yours. Even if you feel you know your mission, this can be a helpful exercise. But first, let's consider the idea of a mission.

Having a mission gives you a direction consistent with your values, what you hold most dear in life. It isn't a specific occupation. It's not something you arrive at, but something that guides you in your life decisions. It informs the actions you take in any part of your life. You could also think of your mission as your "purpose."

When you choose a mission, you are deciding what kind of life you want to live in the present moment, not some far off dream. Having a mission gives your life more meaning than living without one. It creates more passion. You wake up happy and eager to start the day. From this comes more energy. You can get up early because you are excited about your life. New ideas come to you easily because you are inspired by your mission. Your creativity is fueled by your mission.

A mission gives you focus. It keeps your train on the track. It's like a GPS giving you direction to get to the next destination and it keeps moving you forward. There's always a new destination, but always in alignment with the mission. Because you are in alignment with your Soul, you feel good about yourself. You take action and interact with others easily. Resistance is more easily overcome.

Here's a simple process you can do to learn your mission. It can take about 20 minutes or longer for some. Get out a pad of paper. On the top of the paper write, "My Soul's mission is…" Take five minutes to bring your energy back to you and go into heart coherence. Once you are in heart coherence, begin to write the answer to the question on your pad of paper. Write down every idea that comes into your mind. Keep writing. Keep at it. Keep writing until you write the answer that makes you **cry. This is your mission.**

You might find one that tweaks your emotions a bit. This means you're close. Keep writing. Don't stop until the tears really come. That's it. You have discovered your mission.

Once you understand your mission, you can begin to explore how to bring it forward into something tangible. The execution of your mission can change over the years. You may or may not earn a living with your mission. If you do earn a living with your mission, it is important that it is a sustainable income that meets your physical needs. Many people who do work in service to others, especially in the more "spiritual" realms have difficulty being paid for what they do. However, if you are constantly stressed about money, the service you provide will be hampered due to your stress. There is nothing wrong with making a good living doing what you love, even if it is a "spiritual" endeavor. Your poverty doesn't serve others. When you have more, you can give more.

Keeping your mission in mind, answer the following questions:

- What can I do? What skills, knowledge and talents do I possess?
- What can I learn? Is there a new skill or knowledge I can learn to support my mission?
- What do I want to do? What are my desires, passions, and dreams? (Forget about what you think you can have...just reach down deep into what you truly want.)

- What do I hold sacred? What values and beliefs do I hold that are important to how I live my life?
- What action can I take today that supports my mission?

From the answers to these questions, you can begin to find ways to live your mission, to bring your mission into action.

It might surprise you that my mission has nothing to do with animals. Even though at one point I was clearly given the message to "heal the animals," it wasn't my mission. But it was a path to the fulfillment of my mission. I will never "arrive" at my mission because it is a way of being. It is how I approach life and the people and animals I meet in life.

I learned my mission when I was at a business retreat. We were creating a vision and mission for the center I directed. As part of the process, we were each asked to create our own mission. Without any thought, I asked myself, "what is my mission?" and the words flowed out my hands onto the paper. It didn't require any edits. Here it is, from 1995, the beginning of my spiritual awakening. *My mission is to be a conduit for peace, to live a peaceful life through love and understanding. I do this by always seeking to understand others, by keeping my mind open to all possibilities and ideas, and by respecting all forms of life.*

Epilogue

THE COMPLETION OF THIS BOOK represents my ascent from the ashes. My story needed to be told for me to take flight, just as we all need to come out of the shadows to express our truth. I continue to seek greater understanding of myself with new discoveries each day.

Some painful emotions and memories still remain buried within. I allow them to surface in their good time, each mending and strengthening me. I trust the innate intelligence within me that chooses how and when they surface. Each day I open my heart to the part of me that has held onto this pain. I honor the little girl who so bravely put one foot in front of the other each day and each moment to bring me to this point in time. She is the heroine who laid the groundwork so I could assimilate all of me into a whole, loving and empowered woman.

Like the Fractured Phoenix, I have built an egg filled with my remains which I deliver to you, my sister, my fellow Phoenix, so that you too may rise from the ashes.

Your Soul has guided you to this book and to this journey. You have demonstrated your tremendous strength and tenacity to survive and take flight. It is time to let go of the story you have been told by yourself and others. The story that you are a victim and circumstances are beyond your control is false. Just like Dorothy, you have always had the power within to take you home.

We are not victims of careless or evil people. We are strong, wise Souls who came here to end the cycle of abuse and heal the ancestral wounds. We chose a difficult journey because our world is moving to a new level of consciousness, which has no place for abuse, but blossoms with the power of our forgiveness.

You experienced a childhood of painful fire, which now allows you to reveal the infinite capacity of love to heal and forgive. This ability to forgive is pure, unconditional love, the love which is the Divine essence of each of us.

Your experiences gifted you with an extraordinary ability to sense energy, to communicate with all forms of life and with Spirit. You are connected and in tune with all of this amazing world, and your love and compassion for all creatures is a crucial aspect to the healing of this planet.

You are not wounded or damaged. There is nothing wrong with you. There is nothing you need to change. You are the miraculous Fractured Phoenix, a representation of life eternal and strength gained from adversity. Your story of pain and suffering dies in the fire as you recreate yourself from the ashes, and fly towards the Sun.

Your strength lies in the center of your being, your heart. A heart repeatedly broken open increases its capacity to give to others. Your expanded heart allows you to love and help others to heal with immense compassion. Our world needs the heart that has been broken open.

Our world needs you.

I leave you with a message passed on from the Hopi elders in 2000. See yourself here as I see you.

There is a river flowing now very fast.

It is so great and swift that there are those who will be afraid. They will try to hold on to the shore. They will feel they are being torn apart and will suffer greatly.

Know the river has its destination. The elders say we must let go of the shore, push off into the middle of the river, keep our eyes open, and our heads above the water.

And I say, see who is in there with you and celebrate. At

this time in history, we are to take nothing personally, least of all ourselves. For the moment that we do, our spiritual growth and journey come to a halt.

The time of the lone wolf is over. Gather yourselves! Banish the word "struggle"' from your attitude and your vocabulary.

All that we do now must be done in a sacred manner and in celebration.

We are the ones we've been waiting for.

Acknowledgments

I'M DEEPLY GRATEFUL to the many human clients over the past 16 years who have shared their stories with me and trusted me with their truth. I honor each and every one of you.

To Julie Tallard Johnson, who first encouraged me to write my story, and the members of the writing circles, thank you for keeping me on the path. More thanks to Nancy, Susan, Donna, Francie, and Beth who agreed to be my beta readers. Your insights and encouragement made the completion of this book possible. And thanks to Anne P. for your awesome editing and proofreading skills. You are all rock stars.

To my dear friend Beverly, an exceptional author, mentor and the big sister I always needed but never had until now, thank you doesn't begin to express my gratitude.

To my Soul Sisters not already mentioned, Janis, Deborah, Julee, Marisha, Laura, Barb, Jodi, Renee, Cheryl, Nance, Tammy, Julie, Kate, Cynthia, Kathy, Mary E., Mary W., Dianne, Kitty, Beryl, and Heather, thank you for believing in me and holding space for me to grow and blossom.

To my Mother, though you may not have had the awareness of what was happening to me as a child and you still struggle with accepting that reality, I understand. Because of you, I have always felt loved.

And lastly, to all the animals who have shared their lives with me and to all of those who shared their stories; you have taught me the most of all.

About the Author

WENDY WOLFE is an internationally recognized animal communicator, healer, and teacher who has been helping people and their animals since 2002.

She realized early on in her work that her childhood trauma acted as a catalyst to her enhanced intuitive and healing abilities as well as her energetic sensitivity. As she embraced her sensitivity and gifts, she developed techniques to manage her energy field and take back her power.

Through teaching animal communication, she became aware that many intuitively gifted and energetically sensitive women had also experienced trauma in their childhood. This led to her developing programs to empower these women to manage their energy and embrace their gifts.

Today she speaks to groups around the world and shares these techniques through her Fractured Phoenix Empowerment programs and writes articles about energy, trauma and animal communication which she shares on her website, www.wendywolfe.com and her Facebook page, https://www.facebook.com/likewendywolfe/.

She lives on a quiet river in Central Wisconsin and shares her life with two dogs and two horses.